Call to Home

Call to Home

*African Americans
Reclaim the Rural South*

CAROL STACK

BasicBooks
A Division of HarperCollins*Publishers*

Designed by Elliott Beard

Library of Congress Cataloging-in-Publication Data
Stack, Carol B.
    Call to home : African Americans reclaim the rural South / Carol Stack.
        p.   cm.
    Includes index.
    ISBN 0-465-00809-7
    1. Afro-Americans—Migrations.   2. Urban-rural migration—United
States.   3. North Carolina—Rural conditions.   4. South Carolina—Rural
conditions.   I. Title.
E185.86.S6974   1996
304.8'08996073—dc20   95-44535
                                                                           CIP

96 97 98 99 ❖/HC 9 8 7 6 5 4 3 2 1

To the bond between grandparent and grandchild
To my mother, Ruth Berman, and my son, Kevin Stack

If, in moving through your life, you find yourself lost, go back to the last place where you knew who you were, and what you were doing, and start again from there.

—*Bernice Johnson Reagon*

Contents

Preface   xi

1. Burdy's Bend   I

2. Unlovable Land   I7

3. Soul Searching   45

4. Miss Pearl's Purse   79

5. Clyde's Dilemma   I07

6. Holding Hands   I22

7. Mother's Day   I53

8. Election Day   I70

Afterword   I95

Acknowledgments   20I

Suggested Reading   207

Index   2I7

Preface

I first went south in June 1968, when I rode the Illinois Central as far as Jackson, Mississippi. The train stopped briefly in Memphis, in the dark, and then the club car I was sitting in suddenly filled with a silent, tearful crowd. Strangers hugged, and friends stared at one another in shock. The people coming on board had brought news of the shooting of Robert Kennedy.

I spent most of that summer in Mississippi, at the edge of the delta, about an hour north of Jackson, where I worked in one of the first rural Head Start programs. In July I heard that an old acquaintance from up north, Viola Jackson, was back south for a family reunion. Viola had left home and gone to Chicago when she was sixteen, in 1940; her high school graduation gift had been a one-way ticket north on the Illinois Central. In the years before and since, her family spread out all along the route of the train tracks, from rural Mississippi and Arkansas to East Saint Louis and Chicago and on up to Benton Harbor, Michigan. In big cities and in many smaller places along the way, Viola Jackson's kin had stopped temporarily, to work and to see how things worked out, and they had stuck around year after year, even decade after decade. Surely it was clear, by 1968, that they had settled down permanently in the North.

In August, Viola and I rented a car and began driving north to visit her family. In town after town I met hardworking people who kept in close contact with one another, sustaining networks that spun out across state lines and across regions of the country. Over the next year, with the benefit of Viola's company and commentary, I interviewed most of her relatives who had migrated north between 1916 and 1967—ninety-eight men and women and teenagers in all, spanning three generations. A chronicle of the family's northward migration became my first published research.

For the next few years I settled down among Viola's relatives in a neighborhood I called The Flats, in the midwestern city that became the setting of my first book, *All Our Kin* (1974). I had been trained as an urban anthropologist, and I was fascinated by the intricate kin ties that entangled people and resources across generations. I was certainly aware that the people I was living with had rural, southern backgrounds, but

all of that seemed to be behind them; all around us now—
and, of course, for the foreseeable future—was city life.

A couple of times I noticed that children were missing
from The Flats. When school started up one year, Donald
Williams, an eleven-year-old boy, wasn't there. The following
spring, twelve-year-old Brenda Hampton wasn't around. When
I asked, people told me the children had gone back south;
nobody made anything of it. I jotted a few words in my field
notes but never pursued the topic, and I made no mention in
All Our Kin of missing children or of people returning to the
South. Conventional wisdom had it that once people migrated
to the city they never went home again. In the early 1970s I
overlooked the evidence of my own eyes that might have fore-
told the subject of this book.

Around 1975 the U.S. Census Bureau released the first
numbers suggesting that the exodus of black Americans from
the southern countryside to the cities of the North and West
was turning back on itself. Black Americans who had spent
all or part of a lifetime in large industrial cities were abandoning urban life and moving south, sometimes back to the
homeplaces of their childhood.

Before 1970 black migration from the North to the rural
South had been a trickle, a small counterstream of perhaps
15,000 people a year moving against the overwhelming
northward tide that had been flowing throughout the twentieth century. After 1970 the northward flow gradually dried
up, while the southward migration of black Americans
swelled to 50,000 a year.

As in The Flats, children led the way. Between 1975 and
1980, more than 100,000 black children moved to the South

from the North. Most of them settled in southern cities, but during those five years more than 1,000 children moved to a seven-county area in southeast Mississippi, including tiny Greene County; 1,520 moved to a three-county area in South Carolina; 2,600 moved to sections of northeastern North Carolina. The significance of the children's return, I eventually appreciated, depended in part on their age: small children must be sent where there are kinfolk able to care for them, and older children may have to go where there are kinfolk needing care. Over the years stresses accumulate in families spread thin across the nation; after three or more northward-bound generations, a southern homeplace can loom large as a focus of family caregiving and commitment.

By 1990 the South had gained more than half a million black Americans who were leaving the North—or more precisely, the South had *regained* from the cities of the North the half-million black citizens it had lost to northward migration during the 1960s. The Census Bureau now predicts that the southward trend will continue "well into the next century."

Return migration was a surprise to scholars. We had been led to believe that the great migrations that formed the modern states were one-way, permanent movements. People's footsteps, it seemed, were facing one way, as if they had stopped cold in their tracks somewhere out there in the urban diaspora. We had also assumed that people in the modern world, once torn from their roots, never look back.

The people who are moving south are leaving cities where the economy has stagnated and returning to places where the economy has all but disintegrated—to homeplaces categorized by the U.S. Department of Agriculture as counties of "persistent poverty." Why would anyone move from bad to worse? This book suggests that the resolve to return home is not primarily an economic decision but rather a powerful blend of motives; bad times back home can pull as well as push. People feel an obligation to help their kin or even a sense of mission to redeem a lost community . . . or simply a breathing space, a refuge from the maelstrom. For all of us, in good times and bad, the image of home is multilayered, and the notion of return is unsettling.

The South, scene of grief and suffering for black Americans, never ceased to represent home to many city dwellers. The people returning there are not fools; they are not seeking a promised land. They know that home is a vexed place, and they often consider it a virtually unchanged place. The years have not changed conditions at home so much as they have changed the people who once left home so urgently; as people, they are changed in all the usual mortal ways—grown older and more thoughtful, less impatient, more entangled in commitments and obligations, and they are also changed in particular and profound historical ways, their consciousness shaped by their experience of America at a certain time, in certain American places. They have come home, turned their backs on the city with its ready-made streets, and set about appropriating local time and memory and blood and symbols for intimate community purposes of their own.

Going home requires reworking traditional relationships between men and women, husbands and wives, parents and children, blacks and whites—and between people who never left the South and their neighbors who have come back. Such sweeping readjustment is always emotionally and socially perilous. Toni Morrison would remind us that ghosts, too, must be confronted: going home is a journey "to make the past palpable," to entangle the living and the dead.

Over the years of this study I conversed with hundreds of people who returned south, and I had the opportunity as an ethnographer to observe people in their families and communities. I read scholarly works and fiction, news stories and census reports. I came to understand the phenomena associated with return as both extraordinary and extraordinarily complex, saturated with dread and longing, and I came to understand my goal of communicating such complexities as an exercise in storytelling.

Earl Henry Hydrick, one of the storytellers who appears in the chapter of this book called "Soul Searching," proposed a metaphor that captures many of the complexities of return: when you return to your homeplace, he told me, *you go back to your proving ground, the place where you had that first cry, gave that first punch you had to throw in order to survive.* In the prime of their lives, people might return to a proving ground to assess their progress, thinking to themselves, *If I can succeed away from here, I can do it here.* Of course, one of the reasons they may have left in the first place is that they couldn't succeed "here," or didn't think they could—can they now? Returning becomes "a test—a test and a half."

People are indeed tested, in many different ways, when they move back home. They have to find a way to make a living, a way to relate to their families, and often a new way of entering the larger community. They have to change themselves, make compromises, take risks—and sometimes they also try to change the society around them. These challenges and transformations generated complexities in the stories in this book; returning home influenced not only the course of individual lives but the unfolding of entire communities.

In generations past, the conditions of life in the rural South for poor black people had to be either swallowed whole or abandoned; people literally had to take it or leave it. But in the darkness before the dawn of the twenty-first century, as the southern countryside is gathering in people who have experienced other ways of life, who have come home with new ideas, new energy, new skills, new perspectives, the proving ground has become the setting for a political test. This test marks not so much the culmination of an individual life as the chance to start something new, to remake the South in a different image. Earl Henry spoke of this dimension: some people go back home *to better things for others, if at all possible.*

The stories in the early chapters of this book tell of returning home as a personal and family experience. The stories in the three final chapters tell of returning as a process of reclaiming a homeplace while responding to the social and political challenges of the proving ground. The extent of people's success in such efforts will eventually determine the historical significance of return migration.

This research took place in rural, out-of-the-way places in the two Carolinas that are among the top nonmetropolitan destinations for African Americans moving home. Most people have never heard of the towns or counties where I did my research, but out of respect for the privacy of the people who shared their lives with me, I have changed both the place names and the personal names. People whose lives are portrayed here will recognize themselves. Many of them have read and responded to drafts of this book over the years. They see in it not only themselves but me, and in the end they remind me that the book is not only them interpreted but an extension of my own history as well.

Back in the early 1970s, when I was living in The Flats, I was a single parent accompanied by my young son as I did fieldwork among women who were themselves single parents. More recently, as I worked on *Call to Home*, my son had gone off to college and it was often my widowed mother who accompanied me during my fieldwork. Once again I found myself close in age and life stage to the people with whom I talked. Our closeness should be neither overemphasized nor taken for granted—I remain a white observer—but many of the issues in the book touch on my life, perhaps on everyone's.

I talked as well as listened. The observations at the heart of this book are the result of ongoing conversations in which I was an accomplice in storytelling, a nag who challenged and collaborated. In the give-and-take of days and weeks and months—sometimes years—together, our influence on one another was mutually felt; they learned from me what I wanted to find out, and I learned from them what they wanted me to know. They guided me, changed the questions I was asking, shaped and reshaped my interpretations of events, and turned my eyes to new perspectives.

One of the lessons I learned from the stories I heard led me to greatly broaden the scope of the book. Included within these pages are not only personal narratives of migration, not only family sagas of generations in motion, but community dramas, tales of social and political developments that are just now beginning to unfold.

In early versions of the book I tried to sustain a clear distinction between my narrative voice and my interpretations of the people with whom I was talking. But my voice today is in part a voice taught to me by the Carolinians who told me their stories; they and I conspired to understand and communicate their experience. Nonetheless, all the stories in *Call to Home* do come from particular people, who spoke in their own words, and my unchanged inner hope is that the voices ring true.

Call to Home

1

Burdy's Bend

Upstream from the land that Samuel Bishop lived and died for, the water moves dark and slow in the creek bed. The course of the creek twists, doubles back and redoubles, and works itself almost into knots, wringing out the territory like anxious knuckles squeezing a sponge. But at the edge of Samuel's sixty acres, land and waterway suddenly seem to sort themselves out, as though a hand of God had just then and there reached down to do the work of the Third Day of creation; the creek swings out deep and wide, cutting a broad arc, and the ground lifts back and away from a fringe of cypress and gum trees up gently through all the acres of fields. Samuel was born on this land, though hardly born *to* it; it belonged to the white folk, and there was more than half a century of fretting and sweating before he could claim it all for his family, free and clear.

This land in a loop of creek has always been called Burdy's Bend. On the highest ground, in the neck of the land, sits the house where Samuel was born in 1922, where he and Pearl lived their married life and raised their ten children. Pearl still lives there; she has running water now in her kitchen, pumped from the well through a hose, installed by her grandson Sammy, that snakes across the backyard and pokes into a hole in the kitchen wall. Maybe it was never much of a house, but after all these years its tin roof has buckled and gapped, and the framing has pulled back from the windowsills, leaving cracks big enough for cats. Pearl's blankets shade the windows. But the number of children over the years who came to call this house home, and to call Pearl Bishop "Miss Pearl," is almost beyond counting: there were Pearl and Samuel's own ten, and all the nieces and nephews sent back and forth by parents in New York, and there were the two little cousins who came after their mother passed—fourteen children at least at many a time, and sometimes seventeen, sometimes more. There are still children in the house, grandchildren now. Pearl is still Miss Pearl.

In the front yard, slung over a tree branch, is a Chevrolet engine dangling from a chain. The car it came from was redeemed long ago from its rusting place in the weeds by a teenage boy, one of Pearl and Samuel's sons, who hoisted out the old engine and installed a new one. Then the boy backed the car out of the yard, spun it in a cloud of dust down the dirt roads through the neighborhood, and turned out onto the long highway heading north.

When that young man was coming up—when all the Bishop girls and boys were finishing up at school and starting out to work, all through the forties and fifties and into the sixties and seventies—there was nothing for it. Burdy's Bend back then belonged to the landlord; a young person couldn't get anywhere sharecropping on it, that was a known fact. And young men and women certainly couldn't find work in the neighborhood to the east of Burdy's Bend, a part of the county known as New Jericho, which was not a municipality or even a village with named streets, not even a crossroads, not even a place visible from a paved road. The hundreds of people in New Jericho, the Bishops' neighbors, all of them black, virtually all of them poor beyond description, had their houses and trailers, their fields and swamps and woods and winding dirt roads, their barber shop, bingo club, café, and fish shack—but not jobs, not opportunity.

There was no future for a young person in New Jericho, and nothing really even in town, a couple of miles to the east, where the creek finally eased into the river and where the white folk lived and had their paved streets and their courthouse. Even the young white people couldn't all find work in town; the young people of Burdy's Bend and New Jericho needn't bother asking. And so they left. They went to Brooklyn, the Bronx, New Jersey, Philadelphia, Washington, D.C., Vietnam. All ten of Pearl and Samuel's children, all the cousins who grew up with them in the house, almost everyone they went to school with and went fishing in the creek with, up and left.

Pearl herself couldn't ever see her way clear to leave; between her house and the road north were always no fewer than a dozen children to look after. Samuel had to leave, however, for most months of most years, to pour concrete, usually, or do other construction work, on parking garages and office complexes, earning union scale or something close to it, money that could be plowed back into Burdy's Bend. Pearl always worried about Samuel when he was up north: she fretted that someone or something might grab on to him and keep him in New York, and she fretted even more that he might drink away that fat New York paycheck of his. Around home, he would go and have a drink, but up north he was a *drinking* man, a man who headed straight to Horace's every day after work and sat till closing time in the company of dozens upon dozens of his once and future neighbors, people he had first gotten to know back in Burdy's Bend and New Jericho. Every time he left home he swore to Pearl that the day the job was over he'd come straight home to her, bearing money for the land—and the kind of man he was, he always kept his promise.

That was Samuel for you: when he set out to do something, he was just going to do it. He went straight at it and stuck to it and did it, and then he made sure you knew just what he'd done and how he'd done it so that when the time came, you could do it for yourself, in his image. In your muscles, down to the bone, you'd feel just how he would have moved and done a thing, and even deeper than the bone would be the resonations of his voice and his spirit.

Eula, the Bishops' oldest daughter, was the first of the children to come back. Speaking strictly, of course, they all came back, all the time—for holidays, weekends, two weeks in the summer, jobless seasons, times when their help was needed with crops in the field, times when their health wasn't up to the rigors of life away from home on the meanest streets of some of America's meanest cities. Almost always, they sent money home, and from time to time they sent the grand-children home to Miss Pearl, sometimes for a summer, some-times for part of a school year, sometimes for most of a childhood. Unless they died or something died in them, they all came back to Burdy's Bend, all the time.

But the children's homecomings were never as single-minded as Samuel's, because unlike him they had all devel-oped ongoing lives and commitments up north. Eula and the others had families they were raising in apartments around the corner from one another in Brooklyn, down the block from their cousins, two blocks over from Horace's Bar & Grill; they had jobs, car payments, Women's Department meetings at church, a YMCA youth basketball team to coach, a graduation party to plan, a niece to visit in the hospital, a friend with a new baby—and a telephone reconnected at last after catching up on the long-distance charges and coming up with an even larger deposit.

Besides, even with all of Samuel's determination and gump-tion, even with Pearl's never-ending caregiving, even with the pennies scratched from the fields and the dollars sent back home, things weren't looking especially good around Burdy's Bend. Even when Samuel worked the land for himself instead of on shares, he didn't make much of a living at it. Even after a generation or more of prattle about a new new new South, there still were no jobs to speak of for the young people of Burdy's Bend and New Jericho. Even after civil rights and voting rights and court decisions and executive orders, the white people still owned just about everything and managed to control just about everything else. Nonetheless, in 1979 Eula, her husband, Al Grant, and their three children moved home to stay.

They quit their jobs, packed up everything from their Brooklyn apartment that would fit in the pickup, gave away the rest, and headed back down the interstate. Behind Samuel and Pearl's house they brought in a bulldozer and a backhoe to grade a site for a new trailer, and they tore a woodstove out of the old house and used it to heat the trailer. Eula found work at a chicken-packing plant in the next county. Al hired out with his truck, when he could get hired, and helped Samuel with the farmwork, though the way farming was going it was hardly worth cranking up the tractor anymore, hardly worth hoisting a sack of feed. Some days it seemed hardly worth bending an elbow even to hoist a can of beer.

Why did they come back? A million people may have asked themselves that same question in the 1970s and 1980s: one of history's great migrations was coming to an end, was in fact dramatically reversing itself. There were a million stories as well: ailing grandparents, a dream of running a restaurant, a passion for land, a midnight epiphany, rumors and lies, weariness, homesickness, missionary vision, community redemption, fate, romance, politics, sex, religion. Often people tell their stories in terms of pushes and pulls, disequilibriums both personal and historical that perturbed the heart until the feet hit the road. They speak of problems up north pushing them out of the city, and problems down south pulling them home to help their folks. The Great Migration out of the South lasted a long time—longer than living memory, and more than long enough for horrific strains to accumulate on poor people, whose large families were stretched thin across America. A return migration—perhaps a Great Return Migration—is evolving as individuals and families have responded to the destruction of American urban life by calling on the ties to home that have persisted through the generations.

The return migrants have been in their thirties, sometimes their forties, an age considerably older than is typical of migrants. They are old enough to have elaborated extremely complex family situations, to have generated their own sets of pushes and pulls in counterpoint to the rhythms issuing from home. They might be northern- or southern-born, but they were raised mostly in the South, often by grandparents and other relatives, and then drawn to northern cities as young adults. Like their parents, they maintained ties over the years to their home communities in the South, but many of them never managed to establish secure footholds up north. Floundering economically and generally unhappy about the social prospects of city life, they began to perceive the problems back home as challenges, and maybe opportunities.

Some people come home with a mission, determined to draw on lessons learned up north to mobilize their community against old scourges. For some, home is the setting for dreams deferred: the safe haven far from urban storms, perhaps a piece of earth to call their own. Many people return, eagerly or reluctantly, to take up family burdens and settle down in the family circle. Families may still be dispersed;

often middle-aged men and women, roughly the age of Samuel Bishop, hang on to city jobs as long as they can, hoping to rejoin the homefolk when they reach retirement age. But ties to the North are rapidly fraying, while ties to home—which have remained robust in song and story—are becoming matters of public record.

Emerging as the migration comes full circle is a new generation of young people who are not interested in the highway north, who are not much interested in city life at all. In Burdy's Bend and places like it all across the South, country people are becoming country again.

Samuel was proud when Eula and Al came home. He had a house seat for them, surrounded by his own land—the beginnings of a real family compound—and everything ready and waiting. He was proud of Eula, too, who brought back something citified in her attitude, a conviction that she'd learned a thing or two in fourteen years in the Big Apple, that she wasn't afraid to rock a few boats. Up in Brooklyn, she had organized her neighbors for a rent strike; she'd seen the levers of power with her own eyes, learned the hard way about the deep politics inside the bureaucracy. Samuel and Pearl lived cautiously, one long, anxious day after another; their daughter seemed to aim higher, to lay bigger plans. She told her parents that in every stranger she'd met in New York she'd planted a bit of Burdy's Bend, and now, back in the country, it was time to instill a touch of the wider world in the people here. She became Samuel's confidant and was one of the first to know when he got sick.

He fell ill right away, only a few months after Eula and Al

came home. Doctors and medicines were no help at all. He would walk from his house across the yard to the trailer, and by the time he got there he was gray in the face and bent double. He'd be silent sometimes, uncharacteristically so, and they came to realize he was losing the strength to push words from his throat. But he had a lot to say, a number of warnings, long lists of instructions, and he made the time to say it all. To Eula in particular, and of course to Pearl, he explained the dangers of mortgages, the stratagems of land-hungry white people, the nuts and bolts from A to Z of keeping your own feet on your own ground.

One day he warned Eula he would have to kill himself. He didn't say it in so many words, for obvious reasons; rather, he spoke in a code that she didn't figure out until the next day. He called her on the phone to tell her not to worry about his illness. *Don't worry about the doctor bills,* he said, *or the hospital. And don't worry about me suffering—I'll be all right. We know you will,* she told him, surprised by the turn of his talk. He wasn't a man much given to doubting or to suffering doubters.

The next morning he shot himself, and Eula realized that he must have come to a decision before he called and was only trying to explain, not asking for sympathy or reassurance, only giving, as he had always given and always would. He was afraid his sickness would cost the family their land, afraid that medical bills would force them to sell off what he'd worked a lifetime to put together. He didn't want the land to wind up back in the hands of the white people and their damned banks. So he died to save it, and to warn the family to save it.

In death he still warned them. The night after he was buried, he spoke up in Eula's dream, warning her supposedly about the old woodstove in the trailer, which was full of holes and always a danger: go check the stove, he told her in the dream, double-check it, check it every day, all the time, you can't be too careful. She knew that he didn't just mean the stove, that he was referring to all the frightening ways their life at Burdy's Bend was imperiled.

Two years after he died, Pearl was forced to mortgage land for the first time. After the third mortgage, the family's clear title was down to just eighteen acres.

Eula's oldest son, Sammy, was a lot like his namesake: clearheaded, straightforward, and bound and determined. Although he was in high school when the family moved back home, he'd really grown up at Burdy's Bend; Eula had first sent him to her mother when he was very small and she was working two jobs in Brooklyn. Back home he latched on to Joe Davenport, a cousin on his father's side, who became his best friend for life, so close that no mileage could ever keep them apart. When Joe needed a place to stay, Pearl took him in, and then Sammy and Joe were together every hour of every day, country boys with access to all the pleasures of woods and fishing holes, but with something else, too, a sort of knowledge their parents couldn't have claimed at such a young age. Sammy knew all about city life; he'd spent summer vacations and several entire school years wedged into Eula and Al's apartment. He'd seen all he wanted to see of city streets; the last thing he wanted when he finished school was a one-way ticket north. He wanted to stay home, help his grandparents around the place, maybe get himself a boat, go out on the river. Even after Joe went off to Brooklyn, Sammy stayed home, seeing his friend only when one or the other of them had gas money in his pocket.

After high school, however, Sammy had endless trouble finding work around Burdy's Bend. Some of the local contractors got to know him and began to call whenever they needed an extra somebody with a strong back and an even disposition, which wasn't often enough; Powell County didn't see many building projects. For a couple of weeks he worked at a prison forty miles away, across the state line, but something happened to the corrections budget in the state legislature, and Sammy's supervisor told him he really shouldn't even have been hired in the first place. He found a night job at a nursing home near the prison, but the pay wasn't enough to keep his truck in shape for eighty miles of commuting every day. He thought he'd gotten on at the chicken plant where his mother worked, till he had to produce his birth certificate, which gave his place of birth as Brooklyn, and the manager told him he didn't like to hire workers from up north; Sammy couldn't convince him he was really a local boy. It was probably just as well, for right around then the plant began its stretch-out and then the layoffs, and things got so bad that people began to hope they'd be let go.

Finally, though, it all happened for Sammy. He found steady, high-paying work in the heating and air-conditioning shop at an army base three counties away, and he was able to hook up with a carpool to handle the commuting: sixty-five miles to work, sixty-five miles back, two-lane all the way. The week before he was supposed to report to the new job he drove up to Brooklyn to visit Joe, who also had a new job, as well as a new apartment and a new girlfriend. They partied every night. The night before Sammy was supposed to drive back to Burdy's Bend, they partied so long Sammy figured he might as well go on and hit the road without even trying to go to bed. He and Joe were walking down the street after dropping off Joe's girlfriend when somebody behind them yelled something that Joe couldn't quite hear and then ran up to them and stabbed Sammy to death.

So Eula left home, where she'd buried her father, to go to New York to bury her son. On the way back home again, she swore she'd never return to the city, no matter what—not that staying away would help anything. When she stepped foot back in the trailer at Burdy's Bend and looked into the faces of her two living children and the nephew she was rais-ing as her own, she was overcome by the terrors of fate. It was written—somehow she was certain it was written—that she was going to lose another child to violence, one of these oth-ers. How could she escape it? Day after day she lay out in the sun on a couch in her mother's yard and embraced the escape of sleep.

Friends stopped by with condolences. Pearl's girlhood friend Orlonia brought along her daughter, Shantee Owens, whom Eula had gotten to know up north. Except for being almost exactly the same age, Shantee and Eula appeared to have little in common; Shantee had gone to college in New York and married a college graduate, and she'd worked in an office in Manhattan where people wore silk blouses and linen suits. The two women hadn't really grown up together, since Shantee's family had lived in her father's community, Rosedale, about an hour's drive from Burdy's Bend. But their mothers had encouraged them to seek one another out in the city, and they had become friends—not girlfriends who confided in each other or partied together, but women who were somewhat surprised by how much they respected and trusted each other. Eula had expected Shantee to be stuck-up and snobbish, and Shantee had expected Eula to be provincial and old-fashioned, but they discovered they were similar spirits: demanding of themselves, forgiving of others, and delighting in wickedly ironic turns of phrase. Also, at the moment, for better or for worse, Shantee owed Eula a favor: after the Owenses moved back home and then ran through all their money building a house and searching fruitlessly for the kinds of jobs they were accustomed to, Eula had put in a good word for Shantee at the poultry plant and gotten her temporary work that kept the family afloat.

Eula and Shantee exchanged greetings and hugs, but almost immediately Eula was yawning and dozing off again. *It's an odd thing,* said Shantee. *I always thought of up north as where you could go when things got too scary around here. And now this.*

Pearl and Orlonia exchanged long looks and low-pitched rumbles of dismay: *Unh-unh-unh.* Everybody was just standing around, watching Eula sleep. Nobody knew what to do. Pearl finally shrugged and set her hands squarely on her hips; these feelings were nothing new to her. *If you don't know what to do,* she told the crowd, *don't do nothing.* That was Miss Pearl's way: you don't fix what ain't broke, you don't try to fix what might not be broke, you don't mess around with what you don't know how to fix. Let it be. Get on with your life.

Which was exactly what Eula was trying to do, as she explained to everybody later on, when she got up off the couch and started talking about what was wrong with Burdy's Bend. She'd been lying there sleeping, sort of, dozing on and off, and trying to figure out a way to fight back against fate, to make Samuel's and Sammy's deaths mean something after all—and to change Pearl's life for the better, better late than never.

There was so much to do. It was 1984, five years since Eula and Al had come home, four years since Samuel had died. Three mortgages now were chewing up the land, leaving the family with nothing but crumbs from Samuel's lifework. Pearl signed all the papers with open eyes, knowing full well the consequences, feeling the heat of Samuel's anger on her back. But what could she do? The land would not support them; if they had enough money to farm it, they'd probably have so much money they wouldn't need to farm it.

When Pearl chose, she could take an ironic view of her situation: she was a rich woman, with land for her children and their children's children, and with blessing upon blessing gathered around her now. Three of the other children had joined Eula and Al back at Burdy's Bend, one in a trailer next to Eula's and two in houses they'd built near the road. One of Al's brothers had also moved onto the place, and one of his half-brothers, Joe's father—who had driven Eula back from New York after the funeral—stayed on, too. It would only be for a few months, he told everyone, but that's what he'd said the last time, when he had stayed for three years. Less than two weeks after the funeral, Al's favorite sister showed up for a long weekend and announced that as soon as somebody with a truck could drive up I–95 to Newark to collect her furniture, she would quit her job there sewing baseball gloves and call in the bulldozers to grade her a trailer site near the creek. Pearl, who couldn't even remember a time when she wasn't responsible for caring for somebody, was rich in land, rich in family, and so poor she couldn't think what to do next.

Eula was just going to have to pull herself together, that was all, because she was one hardworking woman. It seemed she was never without a job for long, and Pearl was certain that if she would just pick herself up and dust herself off, she'd be bringing in a paycheck soon enough. Pearl had already raised the subject, and she hadn't minced words, but Eula had said, *Not just yet, Mama, I need a rest.* And Pearl had said, *Don't we all.*

Al had worked up north as a roofer, and he could work again if he'd stop drinking. Or else, he'd stop drinking if he could only find some work. One of his brothers had seizures and couldn't really take a job, but he could farm; pigs and cotton, anything you named would grow for that man. Not that anything was worth growing these days, with prices the way they were.

Out of everybody on the place, young and old, healthy and feeble, willing and weak, the whole family, good country people, people who between them had toiled hundreds and hundreds of years at the hardest kinds of work in America, exactly one of them had a steady, full-time job. And that was construction work, which would end as soon as the shopping center was finished.

What could Pearl do? In her reliquary of family and friends, she waited. She got a check from Samuel's social security, and the children she raised sent money for her purse. There was food on the table.

*   *   *

The road from home leads out to the world and back. The people in this book who returned to the poor southern communities I call Burdy's Bend and New Jericho in Powell County, and Chowan Springs and Rosedale in Chestnut County, had not made one-way pilgrimages to northern cities. For generation upon generation, black men and women had been leaving such places, flooding away especially in the 1940s and 1950s. But in the 1970s and 1980s the sea changed, the tide of migration turned homeward, and the story of all the decades in between can no longer be represented as a simple narrative of a people packing up and heading north. What has never been told, we know now, is the tale of the bonds that were never broken; of the ways in which the people never entirely departed and in fact foreshadowed their homecomings.

2

Unlovable Land

Over the years, as time compounded the mileage that removed migrants from their homeplaces, the image of the South they carried in their hearts could acquire a life of its own, swelling into an obsession, simplifying into a logic, embittering one moment and sweetening the next. Embittered and proud men and women remembered fields and pecan groves, funerals, red bugs and thunderstorms, dark creek water, foul-mouthed white bullies, broken bottles in the ditch, and the sound of car tires spitting gravel on a summer night. People who pulled away from those memories still recalled the sound of the tires, perhaps, as a faint soundtrack for a long-ago family snapshot: children, dogs, grown-ups, all settled down on the front porch of a summer's evening, back when the future was only a wondering. Speak of the South as you will, but you still have to speak of it; there is no forgetting a southern upbringing. The intensities and contradictions have nurtured African American song and story from the beginning.

On some days, for some people, memory of the South could run something like this: home of my ancestors, site of my blood and shame, focus of my birthright, still to be redeemed.

At other times the memory is milder: garden of my childhood, home of love's embrace, clear skies, lost sanctuary.

Both remembrances collide in people's voices, and either or both can stir the romantic and the idealist. But as people make the journey home, remembrance also collides with, and eventually falls witness to, experience. Home is a hard fact, not just a souvenir of restless memory, and for the people I know who made the journey away and back, home is in a hard land—hard to explain, hard to make a living in, hard to swallow.

For eight years, mostly in the 1980s, I talked to people who had left the South and then moved back home again. Their homeplaces were in the rural, eastern reaches of North and South Carolina, in communities that by all statistical measures can only be assessed as some of the least promising places in all of America. The U.S. Department of Agriculture has established a dismal category for them, the "Persistent Poverty Counties," and certainly for the past fifty years or so their major contribution to the American economy has been the production of out-migrants. That such places have now become destinations for a large-scale return of African Americans is a difficult fact for standard migration theories to digest.

The homeplace communities described in this book share a certain statistical profile: they are far from big cities, far from Sunbelt industry, way below national and even state averages for income, linked historically to the traditional southern cash crops, and skewed demographically by generations of out-migration. Black people have traditionally made up a majority of the population in such places, though all the decades of black exodus have sometimes changed the local racial balance. My research took me to nine counties in the two Carolinas, but many other places like them exist in all the southern states.

The people in this book live in four communities in two counties. At the end of this chapter I discuss the statistical reality of these places in some detail; the figures tell a powerful story. But nobody, no matter how poor, would want to see the decisions and longings of her life reduced to accountings of percentage points and demographic categories. People who migrate to places of poverty and memories carry baggage that cannot be weighed in economic terms only; some of them have great passions and dreams, some have acquired achings and fears, and all of them have acknowledged, to varying degrees, the ways in which a people can feel bound together with their land.

Billie had been in New York City for sixteen years when she went to church. She'd spent her entire adult life in New York,

ever since the summer she finished high school and married
Hank. She was still living in the city when she turned thirty,
still there when she turned thirty-one, thirty-two. She had
four children by then, plus Hank's sister's son to raise. She
had a job in a beauty shop. Hank had friends in the neighborhood, drinking buddies, hangouts in the city, places to go.
Billie had headaches. Every night, after she'd finished the supper dishes and settled the kids in front of the TV, she sat by
the kitchen window and looked out over the traffic and back
toward the past.

She couldn't sleep; she didn't even try to go to bed. Her
hands were restless; her fingers kept closing and opening in a
way that felt creepy, beyond her control, but also familiar.
With no conscious effort on her part, her two hands seemed
to be reenacting old motions from the work she'd done as a
child out in the fields back home. In her lap and across the
windowsill in her kitchen in Brooklyn, Billie's hands raked
and hoed and picked and tied, dancing around a little crop of
tobacco in the air.

She could feel the tug of old times, old places.

Hank, she finally said. *Let's buy a piece of land and get us a place.*
What are you talking about?

She tried to explain. He didn't say anything for a moment.
A place of our own, she repeated. *Back home.*

I don't think so, said Hank.

He wasn't a perfect husband. Theirs wasn't a perfect marriage. Billie liked to think of herself as a romantic sort of person, full of hopes and dreams, while Hank could be categorized as down-to-earth. Very down-to-earth. Still, he wasn't to
blame, he didn't invent the world, he just wanted to make a

go of it like everybody else. It takes two to make a marriage. And if he didn't live up to Billie's dreams, well, he was a good provider, and she had made up her mind long ago that her children would know their father. So all Billie could think of to do about this headache, this heartache of hers that wouldn't leave her in peace, was to go to church, for the first time in uncounted years.

She walked over to the little church, two blocks from their apartment in Brooklyn, where the singing on Sunday nights and Wednesday nights and other times as well often carried out across the sidewalk and on down the street; she'd heard it many a time from the corner or even the next block, and it was a singing that had brushed cool and silken against her skin, weakening her knees and sending the shakes up and down her neck. She sat on a bench way in the back, and as she listened to the music and the minister, she suddenly felt a lump in her throat. Tears filled her eyes. But they weren't sad tears; they were tears of determination. This idea of hers, which Hank had scoffed at and she had tried to subdue, was stronger than she had realized. She began to understand what God was pointing her at, drawing her toward. And it wasn't the church exactly that was calling her in. It was home.

Hank, she told her husband that evening, in a voice that came out sounding a little louder than she had expected. *We are going back to Carolina. We are gone.*

He said, *Well, I'm not going.*

Okay, said Billie, *you don't go, don't go. But I am gone. I can't take it any more.*

That was in 1973. She opened a savings account that year back in Chowan Springs, and for three years she faithfully sent an envelope every week containing money and a deposit slip. Then in 1976, on a trip home to visit her grandmother, she called on an elderly woman from the church of her childhood, a Mrs. James, and asked her if she had a piece of her land she might sell. Mrs. James owned a pretty big chunk of land and had no living children or other heirs.

She told Billie that, yes, there were five acres across on the other side of the road that Billie might buy.

The land Mrs. James was offering was overgrown, to put it mildly. You wouldn't want to try to walk it bare-legged, and there were places where the briars were so bad they'd just about tear your clothes off. The worst part was the slope up to the road from the giant water oak. The day the man came to survey the land for the closing—which just happened to be the hottest summer day in memory—Billie tried to walk the property lines with him. Thorns were whipping them in the face, chewing at their arms. The ground cover was so thick they couldn't keep their footing. The heat was even thicker. After working their way around as far as the water oak, they pulled up short and called it a day. Without a complete survey, Billie couldn't know how big a plot of land she would sign the papers for at the closing.

But she went through with the deal and paid Mrs. James. To this day Billie doesn't know exactly how many acres she owns.

She wanted to celebrate that night after the closing, and she had big news she'd been saving to surprise Hank with. He was a Chowan Springs boy himself, born to sharecropping parents just as she'd been. He would remember . . . the house she'd grown up in? She'd found it!—the very cabin, and she'd found out that it was abandoned, and it was for sale, and the price was very reasonable, only five hundred dollars. She could buy it and get somebody to move it onto her land, and they'd fix it up, and then they'd have a place of their own. They could live in the very same house her family had lived in for generations!

Aw, Billie, said Hank. *Now why would you want to buy that old shack and all those memories?*

Because no fool but us would want it. We could fix it up!

But Billie's scheme killed the celebration as far as Hank was concerned. She figured he just lacked the imagination to picture the house all fixed up the way she planned. Be that as it may, it was his problem, not hers. The kids were young and full of energy. The oldest girl was fifteen, strong and handy—like mother like daughter. Billie could make it work.

She bought the house. Then she had to pay a man seven hundred dollars to move it about half a mile onto her land. The undergrowth wasn't a problem for his heavy-duty truck, but there were trees that looked like trouble. The man said he didn't want to mess with trees. He took the top off the house and moved it separately. Most of the trees were young, so Billie could tie back their branches, and some were so young even the trunks could be tied back and pulled out of the way.

The truck didn't hit the trees. The move went smoothly.

You got a good buy, the man told Billie.

Thank you, thank you, thank you, she said. That was just what she'd needed to hear.

But then. Then. She looked all over, but nobody, *nobody,* was willing to put the top back on the house for her, not for love or money. All she needed was for somebody to put the top back the way it was—she wasn't asking for anything fancy, just put the house back together again. And nobody would do it. *I don't like to mess with old stuff*, they would tell her.

Hank got so mad he wouldn't talk to her. He went on back to Brooklyn, along with their youngest son and his nephew. Billie and the other children were staying with her sister, sleeping on the floor.

Those were long, frustrating weeks before Billie found Mr. Smith, a friend of her stepfather's, who said he thought he could borrow a forklift from the power company where he worked. He topped off the house for her at 5:00 A.M., finishing in time to return the forklift before the workday began. Billie paid him two hundred and fifty dollars.

The next two years were . . . the best. They had no electricity. They had three rooms and a well—no running water, no kitchen, no bathroom. They cooked outside.

Billie had a job as a teacher's aide in a class for retarded children, but she had no car to get to work with. Sometimes she could ride the school bus to work; sometimes she borrowed a car, but if the car broke down while she had it, she had to find the money to fix it.

The girls were fourteen and fifteen, in the ninth and tenth grades, when they moved into the house. Their brother was ten. They were not exactly accustomed to country life. Billie had to teach them how to draw water, how to cook on a cookstove, how to do their homework by lamplight. The chores took forever, and after all that work, all that inconvenience and discomfort, there was the house to assemble, piece by piece by piece. Every evening, Saturdays, Sundays, every living moment they could find, they worked on the house.

After it got dark, they would go inside on top of the bed and tell stories. The way Billie remembered it, every night a different one of them would tell stories. They had no TV, of course, so they played games.

She had realized early on that if she didn't make the chores into games, the children would rebel against the drudgery and bug her to death. There were some in the family—aunts, cousins—who were bugging her anyway, going around town saying they were so worried about Billie and the kids, off there with no electricity and no this and no that.

Poor Billie, they were saying. *Off there in that old cabin with no . . . husband.*

Hank spent two more years in Brooklyn. He got over being mad and drove down to visit Billie almost every weekend, but, of course, people still talked, and Billie herself wasn't always certain where the marriage was heading. A man can get used to city life. Up there he could get his hands on this and that—he could hustle. Down home it was a different story.

Maybe a man could make up his mind, decide to turn his back on what he had acquired a taste for. But the question was, could he get used to the country again, to the South? Could he wait patiently enough for the people in Chowan Springs to get used to him again, to be able to trust him? Billie prayed that Hank would change. She saw that he was changing, and she prayed that he would realize why he was changing.

A person can bend, is how Billie thought of it. If you're determined to do something, you can bend and adjust, and you can overcome. It doesn't seem to bother you. The Lord works through you; you are the middle person. A woman is a middle person anyway, between the husband and the children, the in-laws and the out-laws. The ability to adjust is God-given. People who are rigid, who don't bend and adjust, will break like the limb of a pecan tree in an ice storm. Women understand that easily enough, but men sometimes take a long while to grow resigned to it.

One day Hank announced, *I am coming home to stay.* Billie didn't believe him. She'd gotten used to him showing up late Friday night and then leaving again Sunday night, pedal to the metal so he could show up for work in Brooklyn at five o'clock Monday morning.

She was still working on the house, which was holding together well enough by then that she could begin to think about decorating it: putting pictures on the walls, dried flowers, plastic flowers, a bright blue rug on the living room floor. Her bed sat in the middle of the living room, next to the woodstove, resting on six cement blocks. She draped flowered sheets over the cement blocks.

And Hank came home to stay. The house was full of sunlight, as Billie recalled, and her heart was full of anxiety. She was certain he did not yet understand why he had come back, what he was there to do.

What he had found to do was not, she was afraid, 100 percent what a person ought to be doing with his days. He had hooked up with a buddy of his from high school who had a 1965 tow truck that was still running and was still painted on both sides with the name and phone number of a previous owner, Truesdale Wrecker Service. Every day Hank and his friend climbed into the cab and cruised the four-lane highway that connected the big cities of the Carolina Piedmont with the resort towns at the beach. They carried no tools or jumper cables, not even a can of gasoline. When they found a car broken down at the side of the road, they offered to tow it in to the nearest service station for twenty-five or thirty-five dollars, or even a good bit more if the people looked particularly prosperous or desperate. They invited the people to ride in the cab of the tow truck with them, even white people, even white women. All day long they listened to the radio and looked for breakdowns and smoked cigarettes and talked about old times. Sometimes Hank came home with a hundred dollars or more, but other times he brought in $12.50 or nothing at all. And wasn't it asking for trouble, what they were doing?

He was taking such risks, and that was something to pray about. But Billie was taking risks, too. In fact, she believed she had returned to the South precisely for the purpose of taking risks, checking out new ideas so she could go with the ones that seemed workable. She was vulnerable, but she had to be vulnerable; that was what it was all about. People had to see her private life and public life as one. It wasn't that they had to poke around in her house and look under the bed, but they needed to see that she was who she said she was.

Most black people, Billie had observed, hesitated to open businesses in a public sort of way. They might work out of the back of the house fixing hair, or from a shed by the house fixing cars, selling fish, you name it. But they didn't bring their business to the front line, to the center of town, to Main Street. They had their reasons. But Billie was going to take the risk.

All the years she had been back home, working on her house, working as a teacher's aide at the school, she had also been working Saturdays in Mrs. Blaydon's beauty shop. She already knew how to do hair; she was trained and licensed and had had years of experience in New York. But that was beside the point: she was starting all over from zero in Chowan Springs, and people had to get to know her. They had to come in twice, three times, look her over, find out who she was, where she came from, talk to her about where she'd learned to do hair. See what she could do. They started coming back, and then word of mouth brought more people to her.

By the spring of 1981 Billie figured she was ready— scared, though. *You have to try,* Hank told her. *Make it or break it.*

There was a storefront coming empty in the building on Main Street at the corner of Court Street, and she and Hank went to talk to the landlord. Billie was almost too nervous to talk, fearful that she'd buy all that equipment, pay all that rent, and then lack the customers to keep going. Hank was surprised at her anxiety. *Don't you remember that other risk you took?* he asked. *The land and the house? Why worry about this?*

Why? Billie wasn't sure. This all seemed so public, for one thing. But Billie's House of Beauty opened up, right in the middle of downtown, after school let out in June of 1981. Billie and Hank's oldest daughter had graduated from high school and could help out with the business, and Billie herself could work full-time through the summer, till her school job started up again. That September, however, she assessed the business situation and told the school she wasn't coming back to work.

I remember a quickness in my hands, from working in the fields when I was a child, a quickness in my hands for handling leaves. It is in my hands now. I can do a head, certain types of hair, and it's the same skills with the same fingers. It all just blends right in together. If you are doing things, acquiring skills, you can't tell where one skill stops and the other starts. When I was younger, I was afraid of everything—the dark, the streets in the city, talking out, speaking the truth. I am pretty bold now. It goes back to the Bible—I don't even see death the way I used to. I am not afraid of dead folk. I will go to any funeral home. I will even do dead folks' hair—it doesn't matter to me. Dead folks are not my problem.

Dead folks don't bother Nora Johnson either, not at all. It's the living who get on her nerves. Nora Johnson will say it flat out, as if it's just one of those things, not a big deal, just an irritating fact of life, like a pricker vine in a fig bush: *People don't like me,* she says. *I am not well liked in the community. Why? Because I have things.*

Nora has a brick house with a sweetgum tree shading the kitchen door. Out in the yard she has a row of alabaster statues, neo-Grecian, bordering a formal walkway from the house to the swimming pool. Past the pool, she is putting in a fishpond. Around in back of the house she has a tobacco field, and behind the field she has a young stand of piney woods, immature trees with crowns not yet broad enough to shade out the underbrush. Beyond the woods is a cluster of houses and trailers where her relatives live. Nora's property, all in all, is expansive and substantial-looking, and it is improving steadily as she and her husband Jasper and their daughter Deborah—when Deborah is home from college—take up shovels and picks and put their backs into sweat-rolling work.

Nora may have enough that she feels the venom of envious neighbors, but her homeplace would never bear comparison with, say, the houses in town that line tree-shaded streets of residential neighborhoods. Even leaving aside the town's best blocks, the better streets, Nora's place is not up to the standards of comfortable town or suburban living. For one thing, her brick house is not truly a brick house: it is two mobile homes jammed together and bricked up across the front and around the two outside corners toward the back. Where the back of a house might be, where Nora ran out of bricks, there is nothing to cover the nakedness of the trailers except rain-warped sheets of plywood and pressboard. From the back, it is obvious that the trailers are so old, even pressboard is helpful when it rains. It is also apparent that the trailers list.

Of course, most people don't have any bricks on even one side of their trailers, and so it is not surprising, at least not to Nora, how people feel. Most people who want to come back home have to buy their own soil, she says, but she had it handed right to her, a house seat, exactly on the spot where as a child she had left herself a landmark to designate her future home. A land*mark*. There were three little sprouts of sweetgum trees growing almost on top of one another at the edge of a field where she and her brothers had picked tobacco when they were young. She'd twisted those three sprouts together, plaited them into a single sapling, and kept an eye out over the years as bark stretched around the twisty knobs of the plaited trunk and the three trees became one. One night she had dreamed of building her house right there by the triple sweetgum tree. And her father had gone away to Washington, D.C., and gotten a job working for the government and saved up his money until he died and she got the land, ten acres in all, her house seat, with just one string attached.

The one stipulation was that Nora couldn't sell her land. She had to put in her will that the place could never be sold. If she went crazy, say, and couldn't get along with her four brothers and sisters, then the land would go back to the family. The land was to stay forever in the family, a blessing to be handed down and passed around but never, never cut loose. It could be lived on; it could be farmed; it could be lived away from and rented out; it could presumably be leased and paved over for a Wal-Mart parking lot—not that Wal-Mart or anybody else could envision a role for the land in the global economy. But no matter what, the ten acres could not be abandoned for cash money.

Nora believed that this limitation was a great comfort for her and all the family. The land tied them all together. It gave focus and purpose to family relationships—the land itself was a family relationship, Nora would have you to know.

I've known this land as long as I've known my people—ever since I was a baby. The path that goes out to the pine trees from where my back door is now—my daddy and I used to walk down that path and see the trees just whistling in the wind. And I'd be picking blackberries, feeling the sand in my toes. We had shoes. But right after school we'd come out here and pull off those shoes, and we'd make a pyramid with them, or a rich castle.

Even when she couldn't actually live on the land—and for twenty years she'd had to support her mother and grandmother back home by working up in Washington, selling junior petites at Korvette's Department Store and living in an apartment with her father and her husband and daughter—even when just to set foot on the land meant driving five or six hours before Sunday dinner and then five or six more hours before work Monday morning, even in those hard years Nora had felt that her land was a bulwark, that owning the land kept her family somehow safe and close: *Thank God my parents made me a landmark. Without land, a person is at the mercy of the white community.*

The week Gabriel came home to stay, his father was having terrible troubles with the farm. He'd arranged for a small loan from the local Farmers Home Administration (FHA) to cover seed and fertilizer, just the little bit they'd need to get a crop in the ground that spring. Gabriel and his father took the loan papers to the feed store. The weather was right, the land was ready, all the bills were paid up, and it was time to get out and plant their corn.

But this time the storekeeper, who was somebody they had been doing business with for years, said he would need cash up front from the FHA. So Gabriel went back to the FHA office and was able to get a "To Whom It May Concern" letter: These people's money has been approved, so go on and let them have the fertilizer. The feed store owner looked at the letter and said it wouldn't do.

What had happened, Gabriel eventually figured out, was that in order to qualify for the FHA loan, his father had had to file papers showing that no one else would lend him the money. So he'd had to go around to every merchant and bank he'd ever done business with, everyone he'd ever borrowed from and paid back, all the businesspeople whose respect he had struggled so hard to earn and retain over the years. And he'd had to humble himself in front of these people and ask them all to sign papers saying he was such a terrible credit risk they would never extend him another dime of credit, no matter what.

So Gabriel and his father had to go over to the bank and completely empty out his father's last account to get just a couple of loads of fertilizer, barely enough to get a crop started. They went back to the feed store. This time the storekeeper just flat out wouldn't deal with them at all, not even for cash. Not even after Gabriel got on the phone to all his brothers and his sister and everybody in the family put their money together and walked into the store with ten thousand dollars.

Many days and miles later, after the weather had turned bad for planting, they found a feed store two counties over that would honor their FHA letter. Prices there were far higher, and things went from bad to worse.

Before that, we had a herd of fifteen mules and we were making it a lot better than we are now. The seasons were better, and if our crops didn't turn good, we got pretty good livestock prices. I remember we sold eighty thousand dollars' worth of hogs in one year—but that was the year my mother passed away. She kept the books and kept proper records of everything—the farm plan book, everything written down in it. She used to take it out of her dresser drawer, lay it up on top of the dresser, open it up, and then stand there writing things down in it—what we bought, what we sold. And then she'd fold up all the papers and stick them back in her drawer, everything neat and orderly.

She motivated us. Seems like when we lost her, we were set back so bad. We hurt, and the medical bills put us in the hole. Farmers don't have medical insurance. She was in intensive care.

If only the FHA had turned my father down in the first place. We could have had chickens and eggs and hogs, and my father would still own all of his land. They loaned him money to get into their system, but not enough money to make it. They loaned him for a tractor, and what they want is not only the note on the tractor but also a mortgage on the whole farm and a note on the livestock, everything. From originally borrowing about ninety thousand dollars for farm equipment, we now owe nearly three hundred thousand dollars—and the worst of it is, when we need to eat, we feel like we are stealing from our own selves—for example, when we sell a hog to buy groceries or a pair of pants. You can't sell anything because the FHA has its name on it.

Gabriel's father, Roy, had left New Jericho just after World War II, going off in search of work with his brothers and some other boys their age. He got a job in Jersey making bricks, and after a couple of years he'd married a homegirl and brought her up there. Gabriel, his sister, and their two brothers were all born up north.

There were a couple of things about Roy. One, he could farm. He was a born farmer, like his father before him, as good as any in the county. It was hard, though, because a farmer without land is like a singer without a voice, and Roy didn't have an inch of soil to his name. But the other thing about him was that he could hold on to a dime. From 1946 to 1967, come rainy day, recession, didn't matter, Roy put money in the bank. And in 1967 he took his family back to Carolina and settled them on a three-hundred-acre place all their own.

Gabriel, who was sixteen when they left Jersey, inherited his father's taste for country living, and he felt he also inherited something of his talent for farming. He prepared himself properly, going to college and earning a degree in agriculture, graduating with honors. He married a woman who

shared his dream, but when the time came for them to set up
on the farm in an adult way, it wasn't going to work. The place
wasn't big enough for Roy and his wife and a grown daughter
and three grown sons and all their families. Three hundred
acres could not support the multitude. The youngest brother
stayed behind to help his parents, and first one child and then
the next, and then Gabriel and his new bride, joined his two
aunts and cousins in Connecticut.

There, in a town that was practically all white, he got a job
as a police detective, the only black detective on the force.
The pay was good; in fact, the pay was wonderful, and he
sent money home every month. But Roy kept calling: *We need
you, Gabe. Come home and help us out. You know how to farm. Come on
home.*

So Gabriel came home, and it seemed he was spending more
time in the FHA office than in the fields. He figured out that
the FHA wanted the farmers to run into the hole, it wanted
them to miss their payments. If it really wanted them to succeed, it wouldn't run up the interest payments so high. The
bureaucrats were just another kind of welfare operation, nothing more principled than that. They wanted the farmers' land.

Not that there was any good alternative. If a farmer tried
to make do without buying his own equipment, then the
farmers he tried to rent it from would always be using it during the best weather. Same way with finding a job off the
farm: unless you found something on a night shift, you'd
always be away from the fields during the times when the
weather and the crops were right and you really needed to be
working the farm. The farm would get what was left over
instead of what was needed.

Besides, he hadn't been able to find a night job. Or any steady job for that matter. This past year he and his father had had to grovel and take a fifth loan from the FHA, household money that they secretly used to buy cows; Gabriel figured their only hope was to have something on the side, something the FHA didn't know about, so they could buy and sell when they needed to. There had to be that little side operation, because the FHA might give you hog money but not understand that you couldn't really spend it all on hogs—some of it would have to go to nails and lumber, say, after the hogs broke through the fence.

Hogs can be so difficult. If they don't eat properly when they're first born, their little noses start to grow crooked and they get scours—diarrhea. You can go to the most expensive veterinarian in the world, and it might not help. The baby pigs can die out, or just not grow. Scours had set Gabriel and his father back six months because they couldn't sell hogs that hadn't yet grown to size—and, of course, the FHA thought they were selling the livestock on the sly and withholding the money.

Roy's best friend was foreclosed on by the FHA and lost everything. One day he went to town and barged into the office, demanding that the FHA people lend him the money to buy back his land. When they wouldn't, he went home and drank himself to death in a matter of weeks.

Roy, too, seemed to find it harder and harder to hold himself together. *I used to be a man,* he told Gabriel, *but now I'm a robot.* The FHA says hop, he's got to hop. They say do, he's got to do. Just a robot.

As a son, Gabriel feels he has to do the impossible. He

could leave home again and go find work up north, which would be logical, since the farm isn't making any money. Saving the farm is not realistic. But giving up on the land is giving up on his father, abandoning him in his hour of desperation—and Roy the robot might as well just give it up. But Roy the man needs Gabriel, needs him till the end.

Maybe next year they'll catch the right season and go in there and plant at the right time, and who knows? If the end comes, it comes, and then they'd have to face it together—might as well stick together now and hang in there.

Samuel Bishop had had certain ideas about how to protect his land at Burdy's Bend. Number one: stay out of debt, a rule that Pearl understood completely but had been unable to live by since Samuel's death. Time and again she had found herself signing papers of doom, in the spirit of self-reproach that swells in times of desperation: *You know what you do will turn out against you.*

That's what the banks want me to do, apply for loans, she concedes. *They'll be glad to give me whatever I want, because then they can take over the land.*

Samuel's rule number two: watch out for the white folk, in particular for a group of timber barons who had their eye on certain acreage. Pearl's eyes were also open to that threat to the eighteen acres still in her name out of the sixty that Samuel had assembled for the family. But she didn't like to talk to those men herself; she relied on Leroy, her oldest son, to represent the family interests. Leroy could make an impression a lot like his father; when he met with white people to negotiate, say, a timber contract, he didn't come across as somebody they could just brush out of the way. When the white people talked to Pearl, they would offer a ridiculous price, laughably low, and she would get the clear idea that they didn't just want to cut the trees; they wanted to own her woods outright. Then she would send Leroy, and the white men would start talking a little differently. A little differently.

Samuel's rule number three: work. Quit your fussin' and work. If you have to go off for a while to make good money, well then, go off and make your money and come back home. Do public work, do farm work, just get yourself up in the morning and get to work. Not for a single instant had Pearl herself ever doubted the value of work, and yet even this self-evident principle didn't seem as simple and obvious anymore. Five of Pearl's ten children were now back home at Burdy's Bend. None of them wanted to go off up north again to work anymore. But jobs in the neighborhood were unde-pendable. And two of Pearl's sons were undependable them-selves—sad, hard-drinking men who seemed unable to keep any job anywhere. And none of the children had come back with a penny to spare.

Leroy was all right, Pearl could count on him, but he had his own ideas about work, especially farmwork. The way he explained it: if you look around at who's making a go of it these days in farming, who's getting somewhere as opposed to who's going under, is it the people who are struggling just to hang in there and hold the place together with baling wire and a prayer? Or is it the people who make big plans, mod-ernize, invest, look to the future? He had persuaded Pearl to borrow money for a new septic tank and a new well. The last time she had mortgaged land was for a big, new tractor.

Leroy's new tractor now sat next to Samuel's old one under the shed. There was no sense in cranking either one up, no way to make a dollar out of farming anymore. It was a losing proposition, more so every year. The only reason she could hold on to the place at all was that her daughter Eula and Eula's husband paid the land taxes on it and the electric bill. And, of course, it helped that she had Leroy around for counsel and advice. He lived down the road with a woman he'd known since high school, but always, if he wasn't actually sitting in Pearl's kitchen, he was on his way over there.

Samuel's final law for holding on to the land was what Pearl thought of as the law of the turtle and he conceived as the law of the gun. She had hauled in a turtle one day from the creek, its jaws clamped on a twig and not a glimmer of a notion in its little turtle head of ever letting go of that twig. The law of the turtle: just hold on.

As for the gun, every night of Samuel's life he had slept with his gun at hand, under the pillow or laid out on the nightstand. When the time came, when he saw the writing on the wall and it was either let go of the land or else, he'd pulled the trigger. Blown his own head right off, to save the family from medical bills and to provide Pearl with a little check every month from Social Security.

What could anyone say about what he'd done? Eula said it was the most liberating thing. Pearl said it was a damn tragedy. Two of the boys didn't say anything at all; they just drank and drank.

The poets say that in places like Burdy's Bend, throughout the South, the land is loved but unlovable. Unlovable but loved. *I can't eat it*, Pearl says, *and I can't wear it. What to do?*

*   *   *

Burdy's Bend today might be thought of as a repopulating place. For perhaps the two generations before current times, it was a weakened and declining community, losing population and economic activity relentlessly, year after year after long dragged-out year. Even before the people began to leave it had not been a thriving place, at least not in this century. It was a backwater. It still is a backwater.

Certain dimensions of the life at Burdy's Bend that people abandoned and returned to are measurable statistically. Data from the 1940 census suggest something of the conditions people were so eager to flee, and 1970 data detail what it was that remained in southern homeplaces, after decades of decline, for people to return to. Data from 1990 begin to sketch the outlines of the communities the return migrants are helping to create.

The striking trend revealed in these data is . . . no trend at all. Twentieth-century life seemed to pass these places by. Economic expansion in the rest of the country and the metropolitan sprawl that came to be identified with modern America might as well have been occurring on some other planet.

For example, of the ten North Carolina counties with populations that were mostly black and poor in 1940, not one has developed a substantial urban center. Not one has become the site of a major industrial project. Not one has achieved family incomes that approach American averages— or that reach even 70 percent of the state average. In a couple of these counties as many as two families out of three now live on incomes high enough to set them above the offi-

cial poverty threshold, and in one county the proportion of
nonpoor has reached three out of four, but in most of these
places a majority or near-majority of families live in poverty.

In 1940 North Carolina's ten majority-black counties
were home to roughly 10 percent of the state's three and a
half million people. But while the rest of the state and nation
were beginning to experience a baby boom and prolonged
economic expansion, babies and everything else were going
bust in these counties. They lost population, both in absolute
numbers and as a proportion of the state. In all ten counties
local economies stagnated and declined as employment in
some sectors, notably agriculture, spiraled downward and
essentially no new employers appeared on the scene. By 1970
only 7 percent of the state's population lived in these counties—but almost 15 percent of the state's poor people.

In 1970 North Carolina had forty-three cities and towns
with a population of ten thousand or more; only one of these
towns was in the ten counties, and it was among the smallest
of the forty-three. As urbanization edged upward toward
50 percent of the state population (based on the U.S. Census Bureau's generous definition of an urban place as one
with twenty-five hundred or more residents), the urban proportion in the ten counties was still only 25 percent—and
would in fact have been considerably lower than 25 percent
had not such a large fraction of the local nonurban population departed for points north. North Carolina remains one
of the most rural of the fifty states; these counties remain
among the most rural in North Carolina. Several are 0 percent urban.

Half of the ten counties lost so many black residents

between 1940 and 1970 that white people attained majority status. During the single decade from 1960 to 1970, approximately one-eighth of the population disappeared from five of the counties; more than one-fifth of the residents disappeared from another three of the counties; and well over one-quarter of the people fled from the other two counties. All these population losses reflect *net* migration; the actual number of out-migrants must have been considerably larger in each county, but the net impact on the overall population was reduced by various sources of population increase, which in these settings would include high rural birth rates, gradual improvements in longevity, and whatever in-migration may have occurred.

All such statistics are essentially the same for equivalent counties in eastern Virginia and South Carolina, southern Georgia, the black belt of Alabama, a broad swath of Mississippi, and the old cotton counties of Louisiana, southern Arkansas, and eastern Texas.

Yet within just a few years, certainly by the end of the 1970s, the Great Migration had turned back on itself, and the old southern homeplaces were welcoming the prodigals. How could things change so quickly? What forces on earth could reverse such precipitous decline?

The appeal of God's little acre crosses all bounds of race and time, but the urgency could seem shrill for African Americans. If security and liberty were to be found anywhere, wouldn't it be under one's own roof, safe on one's own land?

After the Civil War, beginning with no capital or equity of any kind, freedmen began working to assemble parcels of land. By 1920 more than nine hundred thousand black Americans, all but a handful of them in the South, were classified as farm operators, representing about 20 percent of southern farmers. Three-fourths of black farmers were only technically "farm operators"; in the language of the real world, they were sharecroppers, tenant farmers whose operations involved land and terms controlled by whites. But most of the other one-fourth of black farmers were true landowners, controlling a total of fifteen million acres of farmland.

By 1982 farm tenancy had disappeared, but so also had farm ownership among black southerners; the few remaining black farm owners (perhaps thirty-three thousand nationwide) owned less than 3.2 million acres.

As late as 1964 the majority of farmers in fifty-eight southern counties were black. In many states, especially South Carolina and Mississippi, landholding black farmers achieved a degree of economic independence from the local white establishment that propelled them into important, sometimes heroic, roles during the civil rights movement. But ever since the Depression, as American agriculture consolidated and shook out the many poor people in its ranks, black farms went under at six times the rate of white farms. In county after county in every southern state, land that had been in black families for generations fell into the hands of white people.

Many black farmers were swept off their land by the technological and market-driven pressures that clobbered small farmers generally. (Black-owned farms have always been among the smallest in America, currently averaging less than one-third the acreage of white farms.) But disfranchisement and

lack of access to the legal system also snatched thousands of
farms from black farmers; people who could not readily file
wills at the courthouse or who feared the entanglement of
legal paper were eventually beset with problems arising from
inheritance of land. "Heirs property," held in common by a
group of relatives, with no clear individual title, became the
usual form of land ownership among black southerners, and
heirs property proved notably susceptible to tax forfeiture
and forced-partition sales. An heirs farm could be force-sold
under a thousand and one circumstances—what if, for example, one of the family members listed on the deed applied for
admission to a nursing home?

Technicalities of probate and land-use statistics are not what
motivate an individual to pack up a new life and move back
to an abandoned one. When a person who grew up in a "persistent poverty county" sits in a Brooklyn apartment and con-
templates moving back to Carolina, thoughts about the physical place itself, the fields and houses and woods and creeks,
are surely the most straightforward kinds of images that
come to mind, suggesting simple stories with well-paced
plots. But the people whose thoughts about returning linger
on the more abstract dimensions of home—on politics, history, definitions of community, missions of redemption—
have enmeshed their lives in themes that must finally defy full
human comprehension. Their stories, rich with the blessings
of the well-examined life, are in many respects the most complex of all migration narratives.

3

Soul Searching

The people who left Burdy's Bend and Chowan Springs and all the other little places in the Carolina countryside were young adults when they first left home, though many had already spent some summers or even years of their childhood visiting with family up north. Ten or fifteen or twenty years later, when they quit the big cities and returned to their rural homeplaces, they were still men and women in the prime of life. Many of them told me that not a whole lot had changed in Carolina while they were away. But *they* had changed, and the people they had become found the move back home jolting, confusing, exhausting, even paralyzing. The process of readjustment, however, was not just a long unpleasantness—though it did seem long, sometimes unending. It was also exhilarating. When you have to fight old demons to make a place for yourself in your own home, you learn a lot about who you are and who you want to be.

Ever since the 1940s, and in many places since the 1920s or even earlier, communities in the rural reaches of every southern state have had to get by as best they could with very few women and men in the prime of their lives. Few places can flourish when so much youthful energy has been skimmed off, year after year, but many communities that seemed to teeter on the verge of utterly emptying out never quite became ghost towns. Demographically, out-migration of young adults was offset to a degree when parents heading north left babies behind or sent children back home to Carolina to be raised by grandparents. The very old and the very young kept homefires burning. Scraping by quite literally on slim pickings from the countryside, supplemented with money sent by their children in the cities, grandparents raised a new generation.

As this generation came of age in the 1960s and 1970s, they went north in their parents' footsteps. They, too, found what jobs they could and started families and sent the children home to Carolina to be raised. In an era when America's more privileged children were noisily renouncing traditional values, the young people from eastern Carolina, baby boomers of a different color, far from the media glare, were quietly setting out on now-familiar family paths, following the wagon ruts. Per family tradition, they moved far from home, but these young adults didn't even leave their parents: when they arrived in Newark or Philly, they often moved right down the block from their parents (and cousins and uncles and nieces), if not into the same apartment. They were playing old roles in old family tales, but for this generation the old stories would have surprising new endings.

Among the surprises was the geographic profile of their lives. As a recent study by the geographer John Cromartie has demonstrated, in four sample counties, black Carolinians born between 1955 and 1960 are almost twice as likely as those born between 1935 and 1940 to remain in, or return to, rural homeplaces. By about 1990, 46 percent of this younger generation, who were then in their early to mid-thirties, were living in their home counties. More than three-quarters of their parents' generation had been gone at that age.

At each step along the route that they thought they knew, the young people felt the ground spin out from under them. When the older boys of this generation set out for the North to go to work, as their fathers before them had done, they found themselves drafted and shipped off to Vietnam. If they made it back to the States, back to the city, they found themselves in a society in which the attitude toward young black men had taken a sordid and malignant turn. Black Vietnam veterans were no longer viewed, as their fathers had been, as potential ditchdiggers or floor moppers; they were reflexively regarded, with a shudder, as probable heroin addicts, Black Power troublemakers, or worthless, violent punks, unemployable and unwelcome. Even if they made their peace with all that garbage, even if they somehow found some kind of job and set about developing ordinary family life, whenever they looked around them they saw more garbage, more squalor, sorry streets becoming sorrier by the day. They were living in neighborhoods where their children couldn't even be allowed to run outside and play.

The first migrant generation had found steady work up north, often in factories. The next generation came to realize that thousands of those jobs were just flat-out gone, engineered or budget-cut out of existence, or packed off to Mexico or Malaysia or even—wouldn't you know it?—North and South Carolina, albeit to the more urban areas of the states, a hundred miles or more from their homeplaces. (The Sunbelt patina had not brightened the outlook for rural places in the black South.) The jobs these men and women could find up north were not steady, and the conditions were sometimes at the sweatshop level. The North, the promised land, the land of freedom and opportunity, had become the Rustbelt. Industrial decline was the overwhelming fact of life in big cities across the Northeast and Midwest; ongoing decline was the heart and soul of the regional economic outlook. Even people fortunate enough to find more or less full-time work saw their wages fall far behind the cost of living.

The question of how much things were changing back home was arguable—and endlessly argued. Jim Crow was dead, sort of. People were living in trailers instead of the worst of the old cabins. Children weren't scrubbed and dressed up and hauled off to Sunday school anymore, and they didn't have farm chores to do. They didn't seem to have *anything* to do, and they surely didn't mind their elders. People could vote, and sometimes there were black people to vote for, and sometimes there were even black people to vote against—but there was no way of voting themselves better wages or better jobs.

For centuries black men and women in Carolina had lived with such problems and worse; working for social reform was not an option, to put it mildly. Then, for a generation, they had responded to conditions at home by fleeing. The next generation had viewed flight as their birthright and had gone north routinely. They may or may not have been active in the political turmoil that characterized their years of exile, in the civil rights movement or in community organizing efforts. They may or may not have been in the streets when demonstrations roared or cities burned. Their political education may have been overt, or it may have been osmotic, stealthy.

However they came by it, many people from places like Burdy's Bend eventually arrived at a sense of history and destiny that drove them homeward. And back home again, they could not settle for what earlier generations had taken or left. They were men and women with a mission.

When I do fieldwork, I am always torn about when to meet the people who are characterized in a community as formidable sages: should I try to seek them out early on, or wait till after I've begun to learn my way around? I had heard so much in Powell County about Donald Hardy that I kept postponing any efforts to meet him, and by the time I finally overcame my shyness, it was perfectly awkward.

When Donald's uncle, Slim Butler, returned to Burdy's Bend from Brooklyn in 1980, he bought a tin-roofed shed shaded by tall pin oaks and opened the Brooklyn Diner. No hours were posted; as far as I could tell, the business was always open. Out in the yard, under a teetering, sky-high neon sign, Vietnam veterans and other men from around the county hung out day and night, on what passed for a street corner in the countryside. Inside, Slim sold fresh fish, served hot meals, and repaired small engines.

Pointing to the assembly of outdoor inhabitants, Slim told me that I could find all the local Vietnam veterans there, except for the ones who were in the county jail. And except for his nephew, Donald Hardy. *Donald survived both Vietnam and the corner,* Slim told me. *But not without cost.*

I knew Donald by reputation. He was a professional regional planner who worked with several local nonprofit organizations, especially on issues related to rural development. People had told me repeatedly that I ought to talk to him. But they also told me that he was both busy and formidable. He ate breakfast every morning at the Brooklyn Diner, Slim said. If I came by the next day around seven, Slim would feed me and see that we got a proper introduction.

The next morning Slim brought bacon and eggs, grits, coffee, and an anthropologist to Donald's table. With coffee cups in one hand and plates balanced on his other palm and wrist and on up his arm, Slim managed at one and the same time to introduce us, sit me down, serve us breakfast, and fill in the folks around us with the information that we hadn't met before. People in the diner made it their business to pass by our table, sit down and join us, or chime in; they were helpful, and they were also a colossal obstacle.

After an hour of constrained conversation between the two of us, amid a swirl of public attention and interruptions from the regulars at the diner, Donald changed the pace: *I don't know what took so long for you to show up, but since you circled round before you got your nerve to meet me, I've had time to serve up some thoughts of my own about those of us who came back. You may be on the right track. My talking to you is a way of checking it out.*

We agreed there was no way to talk in the Brooklyn Diner, and Donald invited me to drop by the next evening at his Aunt Vivian's place, across the yard from Slim's restaurant. Vivian Doyle, Slim's eighty-one-year-old sister, lived alone in a rusty trailer surrounded by a chain-link fence that held in an old hunting dog and four or five grunting hogs. Except for a little trouble with her hearing, Aunt Vivian and her ancient hound dog had made it through the years in pretty good condition, certainly in much better condition than her trailer, which sagged and bulged and threatened to collapse. Attached to the trailer was an astonishing front porch, with railings and banisters and a staircase overengineered with an array of safety features. Vivian's grandson had built it for her out of solid pine lumber and painted it the same glossy green as her kitchen.

When I showed up for my meeting with Donald, after skirting the sleeping hogs and stepping over the sleeping dog, Vivian and Donald and I sat down together on the porch, within plain view and earshot of Slim and many other neighbors. Vivian may have been hard of hearing, but she didn't miss a whole lot; as we talked, she often nodded and echoed our phrases. Occasionally, an ominous rumble rose from her throat as she registered unmistakable disagreement.

Donald didn't waste time. *Vietnam gave me a new freedom, a new perspective on life,* he said, stabbing his index finger at imaginary men all around us. I read the gesture to mean: *You and you and you could all tell your own versions of this story.*

In the summer of 1967, just before his senior year in high school, Donald had left Burdy's Bend in a hurry. One day he was falsely accused of stealing money at his summer job in the school district's maintenance shop, and that very night his parents sent him north to Brooklyn to share a rented room with his Uncle Slim. Donald hadn't wanted to leave. He'd begged his parents to let him stay, arguing that it would be better for him to stand up for himself and clear his name. But such arguments made no impression on his parents, who packed up his clothes and hustled him right down to the train station. As he waved good-bye, he promised them he would finish high school.

Uncle Slim got him his first job up north, as a bellboy, which wasn't exactly like going to high school but was certainly educational; within a couple of months Donald had seen a great deal of the seamy underside of life in New York City. Slim himself was working as a doorman but trying to get into the maintenance union so he could become a building superintendent. When Slim's plans fell into place and he was hired as the only black building superintendent on Seventh Avenue, Donald moved into his uncle's old doorman's job.

It seemed on the surface like a menial job, but almost all of those jobs were held by whites at that time, and the pay was $138 net. The average person working as a bank teller was probably taking home about $80. So for a seventeen- or eighteen-year-old black kid out of the South, it was a phenomenal amount of money. Plus, you learned how to get tips. That was a system you learned, and everybody understood it.

As a doorman, Donald often sat at the desk and read. One of the residents of the building, a Jewish man, Mr. Singer, would stop at the desk and ask him what he was reading and whether he had read such-and-such a book by so-and-so. If not, he would bring the book by for Donald to read. The first book he brought was *Fountainhead*. Later that week he told Donald that Ayn Rand was giving a lecture and asked if he wanted to go. *Nah,* said Donald.

But he went anyway. The audience at the lecture was white and sophisticated, and the whole scene—at the Empire State Building—was something new, something Donald hadn't ever even remotely imagined. He left that night feeling intoxicated. There were more lectures and more of Mr. Singer's books, and then Mr. Singer offered him a job in the shipping office of his wholesale fur operation. Donald began to feel he was a young man on the move.

He quit the new job after just two months. He and Mr. Singer had a tiff: it began when Donald had complained about Mr. Singer's practice of giving all the employees leave without pay when he shut the place down on Jewish holidays. *What's the big deal?* Mr. Singer had said. *You enjoyed the day off, too.*

But it's not my holiday, Donald had argued. *I'm not Jewish. You closed your place, and I couldn't come to work, but it wasn't a holiday for me. If you'd been open, I would have worked.*

It wasn't that Mr. Singer couldn't have afforded to pay people for the holiday, Donald had reason to believe. And it wasn't that he was tightfisted either. It was just that he had seen a principle at issue here—as did Donald—and he couldn't see any other point of view on the matter. Mr. Singer had not backed down, and Donald started looking for another job. After the incident, the two of them still spoke cordially, or even bluntly, with no strain or tension. But Donald no longer respected Mr. Singer as a gentleman.

To find another job, he approached Mr. Fine, up on the thirty-fourth floor of the same building; actually, Mr. Fine had already approached him about changing jobs, but that was back when Donald had still believed Mr. Singer was a fair-minded employer. Mr. Fine hired him to take charge of shipping thousands of dollars of fur coats and raw pelts. After four months Mr. Fine told him that he was shocked by the way Donald handled the shipping—all these months now, and not a single pelt was missing. The message between the lines was, *Hey, what's the matter? This is how the market works; it's part of doing business. If I hire you and you are not making much of a salary, then I expect to miss a few.*

This was a cultural difference. What Donald saw as stealing, Mr. Fine saw as an unspoken but traditional form of compensation. Donald had a hard time accepting that this sort of activity could really be written off as a routine cost of doing business. He was also surprised and a bit nauseated to see many of the black people who worked with furs in the Garment District making a certain distasteful use of Jewish mannerisms. They would gather on the street corner after work, and someone would throw his hands up and out and say, *Eh, what can I say?* which Donald knew instinctively was a racist parroting of people in authority. He told himself: *I won't do this.*

He moved on to a watchman's job for the same firm, so he could read on the job. He was now reading *The Autobiography of Malcolm X.* When people complained about him reading on the job, Mr. Fine told them off: *Go buy him some books!* Donald said that some of the men in the business who had made a lot of money didn't hold animosity toward him for trying to better himself. They were tough-minded but never hostile. Never.

Malcolm X's book changed Donald. He began to see blacks and whites as really different, though he says he has gone full circle in the quarter-century since. In 1968 he regarded white people as evil; their moral structure had something missing that could never be replaced. Every word they spoke began to sound like an insult. *Hey, how you doing this morning, son* would trigger a not very pleasant answer.

And then he was drafted. Donald didn't have a TV. He seldom listened to the radio and had no opinions whatsoever about what was happening in Vietnam. He ignored his first draft call. But when the second notice arrived, his mother, panicky over the thought of seeing her baby go to jail, called him up and begged him tearfully to come home, for her sake. Her fear of the law had once sent him north, and now it sent him to Vietnam.

He went back home. When he was on the bus for the army physical and realized that he was riding on a bus full of black men, it dawned on him that instead of letting the army draft him he'd be smart to volunteer for some other branch of the service. Water made him nervous, so he joined the air force.

At technical school in the air force, Donald observed very few blacks of any rank at all. He and another soldier finished one-tenth of a point apart, graduating number one and two in the class, which to Donald was a clear case of making a tenth of a point's worth of difference out of no difference at all for the simple purpose of preventing him from ranking first. The soldier who graduated number one was assigned to the best training spot that a specialist could get on the West

Coast, where diesels were broken down and generators built almost from scratch. Donald, instead of being sent there or someplace along those lines, was ordered to a command base that had nothing whatever to do with the power-production training that he had put in for. *I'd rather be in Vietnam than around here picking up papers,* his commanding officer overheard him say. It was an offhand comment, an adolescent sort of wisecrack, but Donald was still an adolescent then, and the air force was definitely the air force. He was given article 15, and two weeks later he had orders for Vietnam.

It was a relief for me, 'cause I knew I would blow my stack at that base. I just couldn't stand it.

If I'd gone to Vietnam right out of high school I would have felt that we were fighting for some great cause and that we were losing. But two years later, from day one I was in Vietnam fighting for myself, to come back home alive. I was fighting to determine once and for all, where do I stand, what do I believe in.

In grammar school and all through high school, Donald had been taught to salute the flag. He had been patriotic and had felt certain about the virtues that America stood for. But in Vietnam he found himself thinking the same thoughts as the anti-Vietnam demonstrators in the states: *If I hadn't been lied to, at least I had been misled. The truth doesn't match reality. The values I had been taught aren't the values that represent this country.*

Donald began to ask himself what he might replace those values with, and he began to read again. A friend got him a copy of Mao's *Little Red Book,* which military authorities had banned in Vietnam. All you had to do to feel you were making a revolutionary statement was to own a copy of the book;

the actual reading of it didn't matter so much. But Donald read it. Other soldiers, his friends in Vietnam, were asking themselves the same hard questions he was asking himself. They, too, knew that something was not right, but they couldn't put the uneasiness into words or connect it with anything historical.

That's where my reading began to pay off, Donald told me. He became an information source, a leader. But by the time he got back home, the Black Power movement had crumpled, and the white-led antiwar movement was in the ascendancy; Donald observed that the leadership that had developed in Vietnam among black men was never transplanted stateside.

When he got back to New York, he saw Vietnam all around him, in the lessons of white people's evil character. *I also hated black people, because I thought: Why don't you see this? I can see it, why don't you? I knew if I could fight for what others believed in when I was in Vietnam, I could come back home and stand up for my own beliefs.*

By the time Donald got back to Burdy's Bend, he was fed up with everybody. The white people who ran the phone company gave him a job, but even though they talked to him about his air force training and his skill in reading wiring diagrams, which few of the other employees, perhaps none of them, could match, he was assigned to work in the warehouse. The black people he worked with there laughed at their supervisor's coon jokes. Donald couldn't understand why they kept on laughing, and they couldn't understand why he wouldn't just ease up and take a joke. They resented his attitude, and he despised their attitude. His supervisors complained that he was trying to incite insubordination. *They would make their jokes, and I wouldn't laugh. I would walk away. One day the supervisor came over to me as I was walking away and said, "What's the matter? You don't fit in!" Something had to happen.*

Some folks have told me that you didn't prepare mentally for your return, I told him.

No one should have to prepare for indignities, Donald answered.

Most of my friends figured that something was not right with me. After a while I couldn't function, I couldn't deal with whites. I would actually sweat—almost like a phobia. It was a hatred so intense it manifested itself physically.

I went back up north for a while. I wanted to assert myself, and I did not know how. My rage was built partly on my impetus to control my own life, my own destiny. I could have gone elsewhere to start over, but I came back and dropped out.

My mother had died, and I came here to Aunt Vivian's. I spent my days right on this front porch, counting cars—how many passed by the street, twenty, thirty, more. For months I was paralyzed. A friend of mine came by and would sit for hours. Sometimes we would talk if I wanted to, but otherwise he would just sit there. Today we are the best of friends because of that. Many folks sat with me.

But others would say, "Hey, he's back from Vietnam, and he's not normal." I was not normal, in the sense that I could not accept the status quo any longer.

Donald got up. He took a deep breath. The lines of his face appeared to deepen. He sat down again. *During those months of silence, I had been speaking in my head to the whites I scorned. I had not been speaking to myself. Slowly, and surrounded by the love of those who sat by my side, I became assertive again. Slowly, after many months, with the help of those who sat by me, I was able to speak.*

A year after Donald's breakdown he was able to begin

putting his life together. He began taking courses at a community college, not because he had any idea of what to do with a college education but because he had realized in New York and in the air force that reading and schoolwork were something he was good at. The classes led to a scholarship to a four-year college, a graduate degree in regional planning, and a position as a planner back in the very same rural county he had left in such a hurry all those years before.

Donald Hardy wasn't married. If he had a significant other in his life, I never heard about it. But I did hear that he had an old girlfriend living in the next county, a woman named Alberta Coleman, who was an emergency-room nurse at the hospital about forty miles west of Burdy's Bend.

Donald wasn't so special, Alberta told me. He was typical of a certain kind of man—Vietnam veterans especially, but there were others. They came back home looking for shelter, safe harbor, but they got themselves into difficulties because they had no way of locking the door to their souls.

Alberta's kitchen window faced onto the highway. We watched a school bus approach and drop off a white girl in front of a house and then a whole cluster of white children, perhaps five or six of them, in front of the trailer park next door to Alberta's house. Then the bus stopped at the foot of her driveway, and her ten-year-old son, Randall, jumped down from the bus's top step and ran to the kitchen door. He barged in, dropping his schoolbooks on the floor and heading straight for the refrigerator.

I watched the bus pull away. Children filled perhaps half the seats, and all of them appeared to be black.

I live on the dividing line, as you can see, Alberta said. *My neighbors and I, we're neighborly. They've got little boys who play with Randall. They're all welcome in my house.*

But this house we're in now, this house out here on the road, this is not what I think of as my real house. You see, I've got another house I built myself inside of my soul. And that's what Donald didn't have when he first got back here. I've got an eight-room house in my soul. And when I have to get away from it all, that's where I go.

According to Alberta, Donald's problem is that he thought every little thing that happened in his life was some kind of test. And whenever anything didn't go the way he wanted, then he felt like he'd failed the test. He had no way of telling what things were serious and what things he should just let slide, and he had nowhere to feel safe, away from the fear of failure, nowhere to hide out and lick his wounds in peace and quiet and privacy until he was ready for the next test. So it all just got to be too much.

What men do—and this is just so typical—men come back home and draw a circle around them, an imaginary line, and they say, "This is my world. The people outside the circle, they don't count. The people on the inside, those are my people. My family, my friends, that right there is my world."

That way will work for about ten minutes. But then comes a time when you start looking outside your little circle. Maybe you have to get a job, or you've got neighbors, white neighbors, or just any little thing comes up and you want to start dealing with people that you haven't put inside your magic circle. So you say, "Okay, I'll let him in. I'll let her in. Even this white person over there, I'll let them in my little world here." And the next thing you know, somebody screws up—they say something hateful, do something, insult your dignity.

And then what do you do? They've just desecrated your whole entire lit-

tle world. Where can you run to? That's your inside place they've screwed up, the place you made for yourself to be safe in.

I've seen it time and time again. People come home talking like gangbusters, and then one little insult and they fall to pieces. And that was Donald, plain and simple.

I had seen enough of Alberta in stressful situations—heated civic meetings, tense personal encounters—to believe her when she said she stayed calm no matter what: *I'm not a person who can go losing her cool. Don't forget I work in the emergency room.* I asked how she held herself together.

I was up north for ten years. I worked in Bellevue Hospital in New York City, and if you ever think you've seen it all, seen how bad life can really get, you go sit around the emergency room for a while in Bellevue Hospital. And then when I came home . . . you know, I was like everybody else, I was hoping for a peaceful existence.

But out here in the country, things don't change overnight. There's a lot to be said for this community, but there's a lot to be desired, too, and if you're depending on what's around here for your self-esteem, well, forget it. What I had to do finally was work on myself from the inside out.

The eight-room house in my soul, that's my safe place. And I've got all kinds of rooms in there. There's some rooms I can let white people in, and then some rooms that are only for my family, and some other rooms that are just completely private, no one admitted but for Alberta Coleman. So I've kind of built myself my own space, my own peace and quiet.

And that's my real home. When things start getting to me, I just say to myself, "Let it go, Alberta." I just step back from it, and I go to the well. I just go to the house in my soul and draw the door to.

Eight rooms would not make a big enough house for Earl Henry Hydrick's soul. Perhaps no single house could contain his soul—or his body, for that matter—because no single shape or size can define the consciousness that animates this one life. He can speak in so many voices, in the tongues of so many times and places, from the spirits of so many of the dead and the near-dead *and the too-fucking-dead-to-even-realize-just-how-goddamn-dead-they-really-are. Wait a minute, sucker. I just come from the Vietnam fighting for your butt, and you been on your clean white sheets for the past two years. I been out there eating rice and bugs. You better kiss my ass.*

But the sucker never hears those words, because Earl Henry Hydrick never says them. Well, he says them, he most certainly says them, but not out loud where Mr. Charlie might hear them. Earl Henry doesn't spit into the wind— why should he? But he *does* talk out loud. Of course he talks—does he ever talk! When he was young, yes, he was shy. Everybody in Chowan Springs remembers Earl Henry as the little boy who would always look down at his feet and stir the dust with his toe and never say a word, but nowadays—I don't think so. Everybody in the neighborhood has heard him talk, loud and clear. *The man I took over to Vietnam, he was a man, but he was a quiet man, scared and reserved. The man I brought back ain't a bit more reserved than the man in the moon.*

Oh, Earl Henry talks now that he's home again, he's not reserved. But his voice doesn't carry. It's a loud voice, it rings with judgment, but the wind won't pick it up. He stays in out of the wind. *I used to work at the prison. I quit, I couldn't take the way they were treating people there. Half of the men in prison are there because Mr. Jones told them, "Do something," and they said, " No," and Mr. Jones slapped one of them or called them a nigger, and then they reacted and hit Mr. Jones in the mouth.*

Earl Henry stays in out of the wind, but he stands his ground. He doesn't run away like his brother Clarence. *Damn him, damn him—he came home, one insult, and he was gone. His bags were packed before they were unpacked.*

To hear Earl Henry's story, you have to turn off the paved road near the edge of Chowan Springs and then turn off the graded road at the curve where the sugar pines grow so thick there's no sunlight even at noon. The road you turn onto is narrow and washboarded, but it goes on and on for miles, further and further out into the country, until it winds around past the mailbox that says E. H. HYDRICK, in little store-bought reflective letters, gold letters on a black backing. Just past the mailbox you have to try to park, half on the road and half in the ditch, and then search for the footpath through the pines; there's no driveway. The path is short, maybe sixty or seventy feet, but the woods are so dense and dark that there's no glimpsing the end of the little trail from its beginning. The end is sudden; you round the last tree trunk, and your eyes squint and blink in the bright sun of the clearing, which is not quite two acres in size, just large enough for Earl Henry's trailer, the brick barbecue fireplace he built, his picnic table, his satellite dish, the shed for his lawn mower and rototiller, his sweeping swath of lawn, and his bean and okra patch.

The garden is weed-free and immaculate. When the bean stakes aren't in use, they are sorted by size and stacked neatly against the shed. The barbecue area is well trimmed and immaculate. The lawn is putting-green perfect. The trailer, of course, has always just been vacuumed. Earl Henry takes care of business.

He lives there with his wife and daughter, but they seem to occupy the place in shifts, as if it were a time-share property—which is just as well, considering how small the trailer is and how big Earl Henry is. He looks like a man who lifts weights, and he favors subdued dark suits, always with a vest and a watch on a chain. He is such a presence in a room that he can sit all by himself on the sofa and make the whole sofa disappear behind him. His voice booms through the house, his eyes widen to fill his face, he leans forward and shakes a fist and then unclenches it and stabs a pointing finger into every corner of the room and out into the next room. The crowd of listeners—present in the flesh and summoned in the spirit, the quick and the dead and the locked-away, the stranger, the homie, even the stray ethnographer—they all spill out the doors and windows. Home just isn't big enough for Earl Henry, not even his very own living room, on his very own two acres, the same land he was born and raised on. His mother still lives up near the road.

His wife Marianne works nights in the sheriff's office two counties over. After two years of unemployment when they first moved back home, she is thrilled with her job: she is a sworn deputy who works mostly as a dispatcher but sometimes as a matron in the county jail when those services of a matron are needed. She drives forty-two miles home each morning, arriving at the trailer just after the school bus has picked up Sophia, who is a cheerleader at East Chestnut High School. Marianne parks the car and goes inside and changes out of her uniform into shorts and running shoes and a T-shirt with a drawing across the front that shows a many-branched tree, encircled by the words CAROLINA ROOTS REUNION,

HYDRICK–WEATHERSPOON–MORRIS FAMILY TREE. She leans against the trailer with one hand and then the other, stretching the muscles in one leg and then the other, and then she takes off and runs five miles and comes back home and goes to bed.

While she sleeps, Earl Henry does his housework, gets the cooking out of the way, attends to the yard and garden, washes the car, and sometimes, when people come around, holds court from the sofa in his living room. He tells stories, explains human nature, rants, complains, corrects foolishness, offers advice, and now and again, in defiance of gravity and special relativity and every other law of nature, steps out of his own body, soars up above the fray, and swoops with the spirits. When Earl Henry is flying, he can see himself and run a commentary on himself exactly as he sees and comments on everybody else, and he can understand everything.

At three o'clock Sophia and her friends come in from school, turn on the TV, and take over the trailer. Earl Henry gets dressed to go out, accenting his suit with a perfectly pressed handkerchief in the coat pocket. He checks in on his mother, does his shopping, pays his bills, sees to his business in town, and long about the time the rest of Chowan Springs is getting home from work, he starts dropping in on people and settling down in the church basement for his evening's work.

The fellowship hall in the basement of Open Door Baptist Church is Earl Henry's office, his conference center, his central switchboard to the world. Seated on a folding chair, pen tucked behind one ear, glasses low on his nose, palms resting spread-eagled atop stacks of papers on the table, he

does the kind of work he loves to do, the dirty, thankless
work that nobody pays him to do but that everybody concedes has got to be done, goddamn it: down in the basement,
safely out of the wind and away from the spotlight, Earl
Henry Hydrick works at telling people how to live their lives.
He specializes in telling them how to live their political lives,
espousing a political style based on pounding away at the
hard and homely truth. When his cousin, George Hydrick, is
running for school board, Earl Henry yells at the campaign
staff to get out and knock on white doors, stand right there
on the doorstep with the white folk and put the message *in
their face.*

George and the others argue back, strenuously, that seeking white votes is a waste of time. Earl Henry tries to bully
them: *Y'all scared? Naw,* they insist. *Ain't scared, just smart. Why go
to somebody's house and tell him what he don't want to hear?*

Look at us, thunders Earl Henry. *Mr. Charlie loves us fighting over
this. As long as we keep fighting among ourselves, that's a powerful form of
social control. If you don't want to bother going after white people's votes,
who are you to call yourself a candidate?* Earl Henry Hydrick, of
course, is no candidate. Around white folk, his whole face
closes tight and his voice shuts down. As big as he is, he can
go out among white people as an invisible man on the sidewalk—a frozen, worthless nobody, unable to call out his
name and stake his claim.

His neighbor Billie has hung out a shingle on Main Street:
Billie's House of Beauty. But Earl Henry could no more
advertise himself on the white folk's doorstep, on their street,
than could the man in the moon.

People in prison also hide and hesitate that way, he observes, *or they would if somebody came along and started asking them to speak their own part.* There but for the grace of God. Earl Henry knows he's hiding. He knows he's hypocritical. He knows what it's like to freeze in the shadows so as to avoid *their* judgment, only to feel his feet in the fire of his own shame. All will be judged, and Earl Henry will analyze himself and yourself and themselves and all the rest of the rascals and scum.

Safe in the church basement, he feels let out of prison, and his freed words bounce off the walls and echo back among the pipes and heat ducts. His cousin the real candidate, and all their kin and neighbors, they all appreciate how Earl Henry's insights and inspirations are a sometime thing. They recall him as a little boy, when the cat got his tongue. They've seen him freeze and disappear in public, in the white community. They've heard him yell and seen him suffer, and they've also heard him call himself the man in the moon—Earl Henry Hydrick, the prodigal prophet. Needless to say, they tease him. *They're onto something,* he concedes.

Why do you think that I am sitting here conversing with you right now? Why do you think that I can sit here and converse with you the way I am? Because I have gone somewhere else and smelled the roses. Now I come back here and get thorns again. And I've heard people say, "Why is Earl Henry so hostile?"

I'm used to walking tall. I don't mind working, but give me an honest wage. Don't give me seventy-five cents when my coworker in California is making at least six dollars. That puts hostility right back in my heart again.

Don't give me a slice of bread when you can let me make money and I can buy the whole goddamn loaf. My mother used to tell me: "Don't piss in my face and tell me it's raining." 'Cause then you show me you think I'm ignorant, and that makes me hostile.

Even a poor white person has mother wit, and he hurts, too, if you try to make him look stupid. So give me my due.

I'm no different from the men in the prison. Many of those prisoners, they've been somewhere else and then came back and got very frustrated. A lot of them have been in the military. They don't want to play the game no more. I'm just like them. I know that I can go and buy a gun, and I've been trained to use this gun. So I'm not gonna take but so much pushing.

Earl Henry met his wife in Vietnam. They were both soldiers; he was a grunt who drew fire, and Marianne was a clerk with a security clearance who worked in a warehouse that handled diplomatic pouches and other top-secret materials. They were both from North Carolina, though her family had left the farm when she was a small child; she'd grown up outside of D.C. He was very dark, and she was very light-skinned, but they were both tall and strong and energetic and developing an attitude, which set his tongue in motion even as it suddenly stilled hers. Earl Henry saw so much in Vietnam that the rest of his life wouldn't have been long enough for all the debriefings he felt compelled to present, and Marianne saw so much in Vietnam that she pressed her lips together fiercely and shook her head and stopped trying to explain anything to anybody. Her enlistment was finished first, and she was there on the tarmac when his plane landed in California. They married and settled in Los Angeles.

If I had come back south immediately after Vietnam, I wouldn't have lasted six months. This place leaves a lot to be desired. The men who came back right away, they started preparing themselves mentally to come back and play the game again. If you take a survey, you will find that they are the ones who stayed six months and who are gone from here again. They are in Norfolk, New York, Philadelphia, D.C. Away from here. Then again, they may be in jail or in the mental facility.

Earl Henry and Marianne both enrolled in school in L.A., but Earl Henry was soon spending more time in the Veterans Administration (VA) hospital than on campus. Again and again he was evaluated for surgery to remove some of the shrapnel that was embedded deep in his abdominal muscles. There was never a day without pain, and some days he couldn't even roll over in bed without feeling the fires of Vietnam all over again, searing from the depths of his own bodily tissues. But he'd have to carry the shrapnel to his grave; the doctors always decided that surgery was too risky.

It was in conversations with the medical establishment that Earl Henry first realized how much of a man in the moon he'd become, without honor in his own country. He couldn't make those doctors and bureaucrats understand what he'd been through, what it meant, how he hurt, what he'd learned. They couldn't understand the first little thing about right and wrong.

How in the hell can some physician relate to what I'm talking about? "I lived off of bugs and rice during the monsoon, I didn't have nothing to cover up with," and they look at me and say, "What's a damn monsoon?" I got to come and pour my heart out to somebody who doesn't know a damn thing about being over there, and he says, "We ought to put him on codeine 2000."

Earl Henry still has a medicine cabinet full of codeine 2000. But he is beyond its analgesic reach: *Give me a job and let me feel like a man. Forget about the goddamn codeine.*

After about two years in Los Angeles, Earl Henry succeeded in teaching the doctors about suffering and monsoons and rice and bugs—*I acquired the ability to speak the truth from the heart*—and he was awarded a partial disability benefit. The effect was electrifying. Now that his pain was official and validated for the world, the whole damn world, now that he no longer had to wake up every morning consumed with fury over ignorant bureaucrats who would deny him the awful truth of his own flesh, he could suddenly handle it. He could wake up in the morning and roll out of bed right over the pain and get up and go to school and go to work and live his life. He got a degree in business administration. He got a loan and bought out the bowling-alley snack-bar concession he'd been managing while he was in school. He bought a second concession and borrowed more money from the bank and bought a third. That third one was a mistake. It went under, but nobody could pretend Earl Henry Hydrick wasn't a man, fighting his battles. *I waged my goals and hard work against the bank loan, and I had some success.*

In L.A., Earl Henry was a man who could sit down with the loan officer at the bank—of course, a white loan officer, at a white bank—and speak his piece and enlist the resources of the bank in his cause. He could do that. *I know how I am supposed to be treated.*

But not in Chowan Springs. Back home, where the plain and widely known fact is that banks don't lend out their money to colored people, Earl Henry doesn't darken the door of the bank. In the public eye, he's a naught—jobless for a long time now, a person of no consequence. In the public ear, in the realm of words and ideas, he's not quite a nothing actually. His stories and lessons do enter the debate, but not directly, never in person—only through representatives who choose their own words as they reveal, or subsume for purposes of their own, his prophesies.

Why had he come back? To show off, a little bit. He'd been so shy, and now look what he'd made of himself. And his mother wasn't getting any younger, and she had the two acres for him. What a mind-blower, in L.A., the thought of owning two whole acres. But it always came back to confidence and challenge, the once and future challenge of living like a man where he never could do that before: *The good Lord sent me home to my proving ground.*

The proving ground is where you first were hatched, had that first cry, and gave that first punch you had to throw in order to survive. Look at it this way: If I can succeed away from here, I can do it here—this is the proving ground. You go back to the proving ground to check on your own progress: You say, "Well, I'll be damned, I have bettered myself," but more important, you go back to see how things are and what you can do to better things for others if at all possible.

Elderly folks come home to die. They come back to make things right with their kinfolks. We call it soul searching. Soul searching is looking inward to what you're putting outward.

Now the average black man I run into, I tell him to get away from here, get away. For people my age, people in their thirties, their forties, the proving ground becomes a test—a test and a half. It's a hell of a lot tougher task. When I came back, I looked up and told the Lord, "There's got to be something better than this away from here for me." But the Lord brought me back. There's a bigger task ahead.

Eula Grant has observed that not all the big tasks in Burdy's Bend, or even all the smaller tasks, are being attended to. *The old community center that is deteriorating and looks like the wind might blow it down, that building is owned by us, the black community. Last Saturday morning I represented my church, the Mount Olive Baptist Church, and met with the community center committee. I had an idea. We have black brickmasons, carpenters, painters, and women that sew. Why not donate one day a month when the weather opens up, and bring boards and a bucket of paint and get together on Saturdays and fix it up? We could do it ourselves. If we don't, the taxes will eat it up, the white man will get it and fix it up and rent it to us. People told me, "That's a nice idea," and I haven't heard anything since.*

I didn't let it get to me. I am going to try do it again. It is hard to knock me down now. The older people need that community center. They have been going there and sitting out there on the porch and talking to their friends and using the bathroom for as long as I can remember. There's even a library in the community center that I used to go to when I was a child. And here it is so rickety that we rent out places owned by white folk for our programs and family reunions. Why? Why pay seventy-five dollars or a hundred and fifty dollars to them when we could fix up our own building? It's ours. I'm going to take this around to the churches and to anybody who will listen. I am going to knock on some white doors. We need more books for our library. There are many black homes that have books to contribute to the library. We have to build it back up as a real center where we can have meetings and family affairs. It is our building, but it is coming down to nothing so far.

As she speaks, Eula moves her hands through the motions of hammering and painting and then knocking on doors. But she'll be doing none of the work herself anytime soon, for both of the hands she gestures with are hidden under layers and layers of bandages, huge gauze mitts that jab the air like boxing gloves. Two weeks earlier she underwent surgery for carpal tunnel syndrome, in a hospital two counties west of Burdy's Bend that had recently announced it would close its doors within the year.

Three years of working as a trimmer on the chicken line at the rate of seventy-two birds a minute had puffed up Eula's hands, with a sensation of endless electric shock, till her knuckles were big as river rocks and her fingers hung inflamed, tender, and useless. When she got home from work in the evening and tried to pick up a fork to eat her supper, the skin on her fingertips, swollen tight, couldn't tell the fork from the tabletop. If someone handed her the fork, placed it across her palm, wrapped her fingers around it, she could feel the fiery pain of pressure, and by monitoring the pain and keeping eye contact on her fingers as she struggled to hold them shut, she could eat her supper.

When they were running eight-hour shifts at the plant, the sixteen hours between quitting time and the next starting time allowed her to rest her hands long enough to regain partial use of them. It wasn't nearly long enough for the pain to recede, but pain was beside the point; Eula needed to *use* her hands, however painfully, to keep from getting fired from the chicken line. What she did there on the line, seventy-two times a minute, was reach for a bird, grab it, pull it to her, chop off the bad parts, reach for the next bird, grab it, pull it, chop, reach, grab, pull, chop, reach, grab, pull, chop. After she'd completed the sequence of motions ten times, about nine seconds of her workday were over with.

By the time her hands had clambered through the motions a thousand times, she was only fifteen minutes closer to her first break and already out of breath, muscles clenched from forehead and jaw all the way down to the arches of her feet, in her all-consuming battle to compensate for the loss of sensation and motor control in her hands. When her finger-tips could no longer feel the difference between the next bird on the line and the air all around it—it all felt like fire, pure neurological fire—she would keep on working by thrusting her shoulder to guide her hand, directing her arm with a shove from the hip. When her fingers stopped responding to the orders from her brain and the prayers from her heart, she leaned her whole upper body into the line and raked the next bird toward her in the crook of her elbow. Half the time when she did that the carcass went flying to the floor, and the supervisor came around to curse at her.

Everyone working on the line with Eula was black. Almost all the supervisors and foremen and office personnel were white—and they were *mean* white people. The company nurse was white; she gave Eula an aspirin and a splint. The company doctor was white; he gave her a note recommending reassignment off the line for two weeks. Her supervisor read the note and reassigned her for three days; when she went back to the doctor about that, he said, *Hey, I can't* make *the company do anything.*

When the plant began insisting on overtime, extending shifts to ten hours and then twelve hours, the company nurse advised Eula, then in her fourth year of work on the line, to quit before she got fired.

Quitting was tempting. The pay was good and steady, $5.15 an hour flat rate. But it was the worst work in the world, galling, tedious, deadening, under bosses who believed that being boss meant being ugly and who heightened the odor of poultry carcasses in the air by injecting the spit and sulfur of tension. The only thing about going to work that wasn't impossibly painful or 100 percent unpleasant for Eula was the opportunity, when the foreman didn't scream for silence, of enjoying the fellowship of her cousin and uncle, who worked on the line with her. Her cousin handled live chickens, and her uncle had spent the last twenty years drawing out innards all day long. He made $5.50 an hour and kept a saucy tongue and a twinkle in his eye that could make Eula feel like she'd had a good laugh even when she was much too miserable to actually laugh.

She heard about a group that was organizing to improve working conditions at the poultry processing plants in the area. Shantee Owens was the one who told her about this group; Pearl had asked Eula to give her a ride over to Rosedale one Sunday afternoon so she could visit with her old friend Orlonia, and Shantee had been out at her mother's place that day helping her put up peaches. She had the name of who to contact and said she had been intending to get in touch with them and find out if they could do something for the people on the line back when she was working on the line herself. But before she'd had a chance to contact them, she'd found a better job, a temporary but much, much better job replacing the receptionist at a septic tank company, who was on maternity leave after having twins.

Eula knew something about organizing from her New York days, and she liked that kind of activity—the meetings, the scheming, the hours and hours of sitting down with people and talking with them, trying to motivate them to join in. Organizing gave life a flavor, a purpose. But at the plant? At *that* plant? Where it would put people's jobs at risk, including the job her uncle had clung to for twenty years? Not a smart idea. The only way to improve conditions there would be to blow the place away in a tornado.

So she took a day off and went to the hospital, where a doctor told her that surgery would probably reduce the pain and might marginally improve the functioning of her hands, which appeared to have suffered irreversible neurological damage. He wouldn't say if she'd ever be able to return to work. But she scheduled the operation, called in sick, and went into the hospital. Four days later, back home again, she felt well enough to take a stroll with her mother up to the mailbox at the road. The mailman had brought her a pink slip.

When you come back here, you see bottom again. Look at Shantee. She was a professional woman up north, and back here she had to start from scratch all over again; she was working with me on the chicken line. When you have to start from scratch, you find out what you really are about. All the safeguards have changed.

When I first came back, it was as if I was in a whole 'nother country. I would try to say something, anything, and relate to somebody, and they didn't know what I was talking about. The more I saw that needed to be done in the community, the more lonely and paralyzed I felt. I met new people, but they were not new, they were just old people that I had met before, right there inside my own head, long ago.

I felt as if my body were moving into a cocoon. You draw back. You ask yourself: what are you trying to do? You become Christ-conscious, a believer. I used to look around at the buildings in town and say to myself: I didn't have a part in making this. I haven't contributed. It was here before I was. Before I became Christ-conscious, I wanted to make my existence count, but I didn't know how. And it wasn't just me. At church I found some other lonely people who were feeling the same things and speaking the same thoughts. I used to want to kill for the hatred I felt for whites. You go crazy. Those feelings were pulling me down.

If you look at the whole, there is a movement, and the movement is not an accident. It is setting the stage for something else. Sometimes whites work with us. You begin thinking of them as individuals, as human beings. Those of us who want a change to take place, we have to let a change be visible in us, to be so much a part of us that others can see it. We have to take the initiative.

Eula's hands-on approach hardly seems hindered by her lack of hands. Still swaddled in bulky bandages, she heads out to the pond for a day's fishing. To carry the rods and buckets and tackle boxes, she brings along two small nephews, a tall boy who was a friend of her late son Sammy, and a visiting anthropologist. They cast where she says cast, and in addition to leadership she provides lunch: corn chips and her mother's deviled eggs. The air is hot and heavy, and suddenly the horizon darkens at the southwest and thunderheads roll across the sky. Some of the clouds loom silvery white, backlit by the afternoon sun, but others acquire an ominous bulging shape and glow greenish-black. The bugs are biting much more insistently than the crappie, and everyone retreats to Eula and Al's place, by way of the cold-beer case at the Sugar Shed.

Settled into a fan-shaped wicker chair on the screened porch in back of her trailer, her gauzed hands propped on either side of her face, she has a confession to make: *I hate to say it. I see many things that have to be changed, but I don't even vote. It is beautiful that we have the right to vote, and this is something Shantee gives me a hard time about, but I am not political minded as of now, because we don't have choices.*

I can't say I have found myself, or that I know what I want, but I know where I've been, and I don't want to go back. I think my whatever it is, my soul, needs Christ. Sometimes you find yourself slipping, and you fall for things you thought you would never fall for again. But if you can still get up, you are stronger. I am a struggler, but the uphill struggle has been much more intense down here than it was in the city. There are better jobs in the city, better housing, running water, electricity, and you have more money. But there is also a racial struggle in every city I have gone to and every city I have ever lived in. In the cities prejudice is covered—it's behind a smile, but you know it is there. Around here you know that whites don't like you and that they don't want you around. All in all, there is more prejudice back home than in the city. Back home you still feel that the white man has your own hands around your throat and that he is more or less telling you what to do.

Since I started to believe in Christ, he's taught me different ways of looking at things. For example, I never have made that much money, but we are eating. Maybe we got too much, who knows. What's the difference between when I say I've got too much and I haven't got enough? You can have too many things, and they can crowd your thinking. Look at what brought us back: basic needs, to provide for our family, and a drive to make real changes in our own lifetime. It all pushes you to wake up one day and say, "I need to go back home."

4

Miss Pearl's Purse

Underneath many of the stories in Eula's family is a love story. Eula's mother and father, Pearl and Samuel, fell in love in February of 1944, when Samuel was twenty-two years old and, judging by all the pictures, square-jawed and handsome. Pearl was just fourteen and small for her age— nothing but a wisp, people recall. They were both still living with their families in Burdy's Bend, about a quarter of a mile up the road from one another.

Pearl was attending school that winter at the little two-room school in New Jericho. Although in earlier years she had been a good student, sometimes winning all the ribbons on Honors Day, recently she'd stopped paying much attention in class. School just couldn't hold her interest anymore; all day long she stared out the window and daydreamed, ticking off the days and weeks till field time in the spring, when she figured she'd leave school for good. She wouldn't be going back the next year because she was already studying the eighth-grade books, and there was no ninth grade for Negroes in Powell County.

One morning, just a few minutes after classes had started, she was still looking down at her books, not yet lapsed into her customary staring-out-the-window, when she happened to look up and, to her astonishment, there was her mother standing in the schoolroom doorway. Her mother had never been near the schoolhouse before—had never been near any school anywhere, ever, a fact she was not proud of. Teachers terrified her. That day in the doorway she didn't have to say a word; she just nodded her head at the teacher and then turned and left, and Pearl and her younger sister Opal gathered their books and rushed after her. The winter wind was hitting them in the face, as Pearl remembers it, and the ruts in the road were frozen hard. Their mother's breath was white in the blue morning sky as she hurried them along and explained what had happened.

Her mother's best friend and neighbor, Alice Bishop, had just died. A fever had taken her so quickly that none of the neighbors had even known she was sick. Two days before she'd been up and about, and even after she was laid up she just hadn't seemed all that sick; from her bed, she'd still been able to keep things going in the house and to order her son

Samuel around in her customary way, almost up until the moment she died.

Samuel, the eldest of Alice's eight children, was the man of the house. He'd already been the man of the house for ten years, ever since 1934, when his father was killed in a hunting accident. From the age of twelve, Samuel had seen to the chores and worked in the fields and settled up with the landlord and helped to raise his seven younger brothers and sisters. By 1944 both of his brothers and two of his sisters were already grown and gone, working at war jobs in New York and New Jersey. As soon as the kids got big enough to be some help around the place, it seemed, they always left. They sent money home, but still, Samuel felt the weight of his situation.

He had so much responsibility that the draft board left him alone. But that cold February morning, when he got out of bed and stirred the fire in the stove in absolute silence, with his mother suddenly too weak to fuss at him, he had more responsibility than he could bear. He woke up the three little girls and sent them to school. Then he went over to his mother's bed and couldn't rouse her. He ran all the way to Pearl's house, where he told Pearl's mother and then lay his head down on the table.

Samuel's three youngest sisters had been sitting in the schoolroom that morning with Pearl and Opal, but Pearl's mother did not tell them of the tragedy or take them home. She had left them there at their desks to finish out the school day, to live one last regular day before orphanhood took over their lives. Things were not ready for them just yet. Pearl and her sister and her mother had washed Alice's body and laid her out. They had scrubbed the house clean and fixed supper.

The girls came home from school and burst into tears. Samuel walked in, and the first thing he noticed was Pearl trying to comfort his little sisters. *She's here to help*, he thought. *There is somebody who has come to help.*

You couldn't call it love at first sight, since this was far from his first sight of Pearl. They were near neighbors, and their mothers had been close friends. She'd been just a little girl all these years, the age of his baby sisters. If it wasn't love at first sight, still, it was love at first notice. What Samuel first noticed about Pearl was how quiet and calm she was, in a house full of weeping, and how she just pitched in, digging into the work. Fifty years later Pearl would recall: *He trusted me more than I trusted myself.* She would also say: *Ever since I've been knowing myself, I've been taking care of somebody.*

Within a little over a year, all three of Samuel's youngest sisters had left home, joining their brothers and sisters up north. Samuel stayed on alone in the house at Burdy's Bend. He and Pearl were married in June 1945, just after Pearl's sixteenth birthday. In October of that year, when Pearl was pregnant with Eula, Samuel went up to the Bronx for the first time, to work tending an incinerator in a union job his brother had arranged. By the following April he had quit that job and was back home to set out tobacco, thus starting the pattern of seasons and off-seasons that would set the rhythm of the rest of his life.

When he came back home, there were three babies in the house at Burdy's Bend: their daughter Eula and two nephews, the sons of one of Samuel's sisters. The next spring there was also their newborn son Leroy. Eventually there would be ten children of their own—from Eula born in 1946 to Mary born in 1965—and there would always be other children in the house as well. The house had four bedrooms and a sleeping porch and no rooms that weren't bedrooms; the living room was a bedroom, and so was the kitchen.

There was no bathroom. There was no outhouse. There was a slop jar, and Samuel believed that one of his personal duties as the protector of his family was to carry out the jar himself. Children shouldn't have to do that kind of thing. Samuel wanted his children to be happy.

He was a good provider; not a single day went by that all those children didn't have food to eat. They didn't always have new shoes and nice clothes—everything was scarce, always. But day in and day out, no matter what, there was always something for dinner.

Pearl was so young when they married that he had to teach her how to cook. She had so many children, one after the other, that he felt he had to help change diapers, feed the babies, wash them, dry them, get after them when they did wrong. He didn't believe in sitting around while Pearl or anybody else kept on working, and he had a certain patience with children. When he showed up, they came from all directions to play ball with him, to wrestle, to have a race up to the road and back. On Saturdays, when he was home during the summer, he would load the kids up on the pickup and give them a whole day to themselves. *With them children,* Pearl recalls, *he was just like a woman.*

The summer I was pregnant with my tenth child, I gathered sassafras root bark and dried it and made summer tea. I was sitting there reading a library book to the kids when I felt that pain. I had a ripe pain. I told the kids quickly, "Now! It's time to go to bed—now!" When they had gone, I got it again. Samuel was about to get the midwife when I put both hands here and I couldn't do nothing but go on and have the baby. I shot that girl down to the foot of the bed. Once again the midwife didn't make it. Samuel took good care of me. He put on clean sheets and made us some sassafras tea.

Samuel wasn't always around to carry out the slop jar and help deliver babies and brew sassafras tea. Sometimes he was drinking; he wasn't the type to get mean when he drank, like the man who'd married Pearl's girlfriend Orlonia, and he managed to tend to his work even during bouts with the bottle. But still, after a few beers he could seem blind to the people around him. Drinking or not drinking, for long months of almost every year he was off in New York or New Jersey, usually pouring concrete for highways and parking decks. He went north every fall, when the birds and vacationers were headed south, and he worked till winter weather shut down construction. Sometimes he found jobs that kept going through the winter, and sometimes he found work that was on-again off-again during the cold months, depending on the weather. His original plan was to return to Burdy's Bend each spring in time for planting season, but that proved impossible over the long run; some years it was clear that his boss would hold it against him at hiring time the next fall if he quit a job before it was completed. Some years his children and cousins and nephews pitched in when he couldn't make it home in time to get in a crop; in other years, for various reasons, planting time came and went without any planting at Burdy's Bend. For three years straight Samuel wasn't home for more than a few days at a time, and he became an absentee landlord, barking orders to his farm laborers over the phone.

There was a lot of farmwork, and with no plumbing in the house and no money, the chores were endless. The children had to pitch in, and Pearl and Samuel had to keep after them. Burdy's Bend was no place for shirkers. When Samuel was home, he disciplined the children, particularly the older ones, particularly the boys. When he was away, all the correcting, as well as all the chores, fell on Pearl. Looking back, she feared she may have been too hard on the children. She had expected so much, from such small children. Some of the nieces and nephews would cry for their mothers. But then again, when they went up north to visit their parents during the summers, they would cry for Miss Pearl. They would get on the phone every day to talk to her.

My mother had a way with children, Eula recalled. In the winters, when my father was away, she could always think of something to keep us all entertained—games, Bible stories, something. We would go get a library book and just bawl for her to read it to us. She took every one of us to church. There was something about her. People knew, if there was a child that needed a mother, Miss Pearl was somebody they could count on.

For some of the children she took in, Miss Pearl was their only mother. Death and hard times, she says, were all around them. Samuel's two brothers, Abraham and Saul, were both widowed within a few months of each other, leaving twelve children motherless. Abraham had brought his family back to Burdy's Bend three months before his wife died, hoping that country air would improve her health, and hoping also that the folks back home could help him take care of her and the children. After Saul's wife was killed in a car accident on the New Jersey Turnpike, the two brothers decided to try to make a go of it with all their children together in Abraham's house, about a mile down the road from Pearl and Samuel's place. Quickly, life went from very bad to much worse for the two widowed men and the twelve motherless children: the house burned down. No getting around it after that—the men had to go back to the city to work, and the children had to be split up and parceled out. Pearl wound up with five of them for a while, and she kept the two youngest—Joyce and Jimmy—for sixteen years. *I do feel sorry for those children whose mother is dead,* she recalled.

But you can't let nothing like that get in the child's way. You got to raise 'em. You can't let them feel sorry for themselves. A lot of children never seen their mother, but they got to be raised. They got to be disciplined. You got to try to do what you can for them. There is enough that stands in their way. Jimmy, for example, he takes after his side of the family in that he's got sugar—he's got it bad. But he's still better off than Joyce. That girl never seem right. Ever since her mother died and her father went north and that house got burned up, she seem like she in another world. That was a long time ago, but I still can't seem to reach her.

The first time I saw Joyce I was not allowed to meet her; when she entered the room, Miss Pearl escorted me out-doors, whispering that Joyce had no sense and should not be interviewed. The second time I saw her she sat at the far end of the house with her face locked up tight, brows beetled, and didn't say a word. It was clear I was a long way from a conversation with her.

The third time we saw one another, at Jimmy's daughter's birthday party, we still didn't talk. We didn't have much opportunity, because soon after Joyce arrived she stalked out of the room. Miss Pearl had mumbled something I couldn't quite make out, a remark that apparently referred to Joyce's drinking. I followed her out into the yard where the children were playing, and though she continued to ignore me, she was notably animated and playful with the children, joining in their games, laughing and joking with them, literally leaping back and forth across a ditch. She is a tiny woman, slight to the point of looking frail, but at the children's party she looked wiry and energetic, physically childlike.

Joyce is thirty-five years old, however, and has no children. She lives by herself in the woods, in a one-room cabin behind her brother's trailer. After the birthday party, Jimmy told me he was a nervous wreck because she and her boyfriend had been fighting so much that neighbors had started calling him to complain. Pearl said Joyce didn't have the faintest idea how to manage her life or her money: *She's just purely self-destructive.* Then it emerged that Joyce had been interrogating people in the community about my project, inquiring at length into the details of my interviewing. I don't know what they told her, but a few days later a note appeared on the seat of my car inviting me to come by her place. The note had a P.S.: "Bring a fishing pole."

When I showed up, picnic lunch in hand, we didn't stop to talk but headed straight through the woods to Heckert's Pond, tromping through the underbrush, ducking under barbed wire, dodging poison ivy. Any notion of a frail or delicate Joyce quickly evaporated. My memory of a sullen, worried, jittery Joyce also had to be set aside: away from her brother and her aunt and all the rest of the family, she was calm and pleasant, making small talk about the dogwood blooms and the birdsong she liked to listen to at sunrise. Her face was soft and relaxed, even smiling.

At the edge of the pond, as I swatted mosquitoes and she baited her hooks, she suddenly turned to me and asked what I was trying to find out in Burdy's Bend. She said she'd heard I was talking to people who'd come back from the city—why was I so interested in such a thing?

I told her I was curious about how people and places change. Her eyelids slowly opened wide.

The only thing I ever wanted out of life was a husband and a nice home and maybe a couple kids—the average everyday housewife and mother. That was the only thing I was looking for. But I didn't get it.

I didn't have a mother nor a father. My mother died when I was three, and my father left. My Aunt Pearl—I kind of idolized her really. I thought she was perfect. Now I know that she is not perfect, and she won't ever be perfect. But what she had, a husband, a family, that seemed to me to be the perfect thing. Something like her life, that was what I always dreamed of. I didn't want so much to be like her, but I wanted it to be the same—the security, the warmth. And that I wouldn't feel alone anymore.

So old Whit came down from New York, and I fell in love with him. He came down here sweet-talking, you know, and I just had to have him. He was the sweetest thing. I just had to get him. He was everything to me.

Things were so rough for me at home, the way I come up. Nobody taught me nothing—I even had to teach myself to cook, teach myself to clean. And when I should have been in school, I had to go into the tobacco field. Miss Pearl never taught me. She never even hugged me the whole time I was growing up, never gave me that physical contact. It's true, she never, ever hugged me but for one single time. And I don't know why she did it that one time—I think her son was back home and she was happy about that, and she just walked up to me and put her arms around me. And with my cousins, I couldn't ever talk to them really, because they were doing for me when my father left me. I couldn't talk to them about how mean they were to me. I was eating their bread and butter.

Everything I did, it wasn't good enough for Aunt Pearl. If I expressed myself, I was wrong. I always wanted to be the perfect child. I couldn't do enough to please Miss Pearl. But regardless, it wasn't enough. It was so painful. It's a scar you never outgrow. I grew up thinking that I am not going to be anything.

All my life was governed by what my aunt would say or what my brother would say. I was always trying to please my aunt, please my brother, please my cousins, please everybody in the world except for Joyce. I wish my aunt would have talked about what I could do, what I could be, because I didn't have no idea, no plan in my life. I was so inexperienced. But all Miss Pearl ever talked to me about was how I was going to be pregnant before I was thirteen. And here I am past thirty and still not pregnant. I just never got any self-confidence at home.

My whole life was church. Now, nobody forced me and made me go to church. I was spiritual. But that was all I knew how to do—I knew how to sing in the choir, how to go to Sunday school. I didn't even know how to talk to people, except for at home and at church. I never had any experience even talking to anybody else.

And then old Whit came along, and he was from the city—from the street, you could say. And maybe I could have seen, if I had had enough time. But everybody was putting pressure on me: "He's no good, Joyce," "You deserve better, Joyce." And I'm all accustomed to listening to what they say. I couldn't really give myself a chance to find out for myself. It seemed like everybody was controlling Joyce but Joyce.

So I left home and went up to New York to be with him. All right. We shacked up. He used me. Until I got tired of being used, and then I left.

I moved in with my sister, and I met this other man, Bernard. Now, he wasn't the one for me either, because he was married. But it was still security for me, I felt protected. I didn't have anybody to turn to, and Bernard was telling me, "You better get a job. You're throwing your life away." He was nice to me. He was almost more of a father than a lover. But I was just so unhappy, because living with a man, just being with him, that wasn't what I wanted. I wasn't the type to want to go to college and be a doctor and a nurse. I just wanted to get married. So I got tired of Bernard, and I left him, too.

I still love him to a certain extent. I still love Whit especially. I'm the type of person, I can see a wino on the street and think there's some good in him, something to love. Everybody say I'm crazy, but I don't see nothing wrong with it.

In New York, Joyce found work cleaning houses and eventually took a full-time position in the home of a wealthy Jewish family—a father, mother, and two children. One day she walked in on a suicide attempt by the mother. *Lady, you is a fool!* screamed Joyce. *You are living in all this luxury, this beauty, and here I am trying to help you, and my apartment is rich in cockroaches.* She kept on talking, held the woman's hand, stayed by her side until the crisis passed. The woman's son said later that Joyce had turned his mother around that day and saved her life.

But when she got back to her own apartment, panic struck: *Oh, my God, my God, what have I done? I just said this, said that, to a white woman, and she could have me fired, have me killed or something. What have I done?*

What happened next was an experience that Joyce would later term a nervous breakdown. She lay in bed for two weeks, anguishing over her outburst. What had gotten into her? How could she have talked that way? At the end of the two weeks, what she realized was that for the first time in her life she had found her own voice, had spoken out for her own self, not trying to please Miss Pearl or Whit or anybody else any longer. Just speaking out in the bold new voice of Joyce herself.

She packed her things and moved back to Burdy's Bend.

I've made three hard decisions in my life. First one was leaving home. I was so unexperienced. I had no communication with any outside individual. So I was fearful. I didn't know how to do anything. My education wasn't that good. So that was one hard decision.

Then another one was depending on men. When I left home, I had to depend on men to a certain extent, because I really couldn't do for myself. And I had to decide if they were doing the right thing by me, or they were just using me, or whether they loved me or what. It was a tough decision to let them take care of me. I struggled with it. I was scared to accept help from them. The way I thought was, hey, you are supposed to be married, and a young girl ain't supposed to do this. How in the hell is she going to make it? But I think it depends on the individual. There is some nice males out there that will help you and look out for your best interest and will not take advantage of you. They is very hard to find, you have to be very careful. Someone will use you, and cows will come home. Someone will use you to death.

Then my other hard decision was coming home. Will they accept me? How will they accept me? With open arms and love, or as being a failure? You know, "Okay, you went up to New York, and what did you accomplish? You didn't do a doggone thing." Usually, when you come back from New York, especially after all these years, you are supposed to come back with a bundle of money and set yourself a house. And you know, when you get home, the men are going to come around and beg.

But being away was the best thing that ever happened to me. It gave me the chance to grow with experience. The old Joyce wouldn't be here with you, wouldn't talk to you. I still have fear, and I probably will always have fear. But what I feel is, I have passed through the storm. The worst is behind me now.

The new Joyce that I became after that, I just knew she was beautiful. I was just like a song. I was love, I was a doll, I had something going— really. I discovered I could be somebody if I wanted to.

Aunt Pearl hasn't changed. She is exactly the same, nosy as ever. She and Eula both don't know how to mind their own business. And it seems like them two, and Jimmy and the others, they all take me as a joke: "Oh, crazy old Joyce. She can get herself into the craziest situations." Which I can, really. But I'm trying to do things different by my nieces and nephews. I hug them every day, every chance I get I give them that affection. I tell them how they're precious, there's so much they can do in life, don't get discouraged. If I'd have gotten self-confidence like that when I was at home, there's no telling what I could have done up in New York.

But nobody here . . . it doesn't seem like there's anybody at all I can talk to. Now, it's true I can always talk to God—that's something else I discovered. I started talking to him. And it's really helped me. I wouldn't tell you no lie.

But all they say is: "Crazy old Joyce, and now she's already into heaven." I've given up on trying to please them a long time ago.

Jimmy Bishop looks just like his little sister: loose-jointed and slight of frame, with a face touched by childlike expressions. He and Joyce have the same eyebrows, especially— movable brows that can clamp down tight or leap open wide, on a forehead that can furrow up one minute and ease completely smooth the next.

Jimmy and Joyce grew up together, struggling with the

same tragedies and difficult times, surrounded by the same people, attending the same schools, hearing the same stories. They both yearned for families of their own modeled after the example of Pearl and Samuel. They both went north the same summer—Jimmy was eighteen, Joyce seventeen—and they both returned home around the same time, about fifteen years later. *Seems like everybody around here left home at one time,* Jimmy has observed, *and a great majority of people came back about the same time.*

Brother and sister still live essentially together, in homes on the same property, within a couple of hundred yards of one another. But their lives have been so different, and remain so different, that they might as well have taken place on different planets.

One difference was Mr. McKinney. Joyce never knew him, but he taught Jimmy for three years at New Jericho High School. He taught bricklaying and stone masonry, and for students who paid attention—as he never tired of telling them—he offered a shot at the future. The future for which Mr. McKinney was preparing his boys couldn't be realized at home in Powell County or anywhere nearby, but if young people would just take what he taught them and hit the road like gypsies, as he put it, moving with the seasons and the economic cycles between Richmond, Washington, D.C., New Jersey, and points between, then they would have a real shot at the good life, at the American dream. Jimmy for one was ready to give it his best shot.

When he was eighteen, he married Daisy, from down the road, and took off for Baltimore. He had an older brother there, and his father was in Wilmington, Delaware, a short train ride away. Jimmy looked forward to spending time with his father, getting to know him. The way he looked at it, his father had always been a real father, a real man, off working to support the family. True, he wasn't around when Jimmy and Joyce were growing up—they never got to see him for more than a few days at a time—but it wasn't like he'd abandoned them, far from it. He sent money to Miss Pearl, and this was the way it had to be, the right way for a man like him with a family. Then, too, Uncle Samuel did pretty much the same thing, leaving Miss Pearl and them to go work and support them. When he first got married, Jimmy took the same approach. He left Daisy at home with her parents while he went north to lay brick.

He and his father spent many weekends together that first year, but the companionship didn't come close to compensating for how much he missed Daisy. He began rushing home on weekends, driving all night, to be with her. But he was all by himself in Baltimore the day their baby was born, and he couldn't even think of his new little girl, Tonesha, without feeling sick about being so far away from her.

His own father had always been away. Uncle Samuel had been around more, but he was odd, he wasn't always there when he seemed to be there. One time, when Jimmy was small, he had noticed Samuel coming across the yard, and he'd run up to greet him: *Hi'ya, Uncle Sam.* His uncle had walked right on by, as if Jimmy were invisible. He decided things would be different for Tonesha; her father would *be there* for her.

He brought Daisy and the baby up north to be with him. They moved to Newark, at first staying in his uncle's apartment and then getting a place of their own—on their own, as Jimmy put it, but not at all alone. His father wasn't far away, two sisters (one was Joyce) lived in the Bronx, and there was the brother down in Baltimore. They alternated weekends: one weekend they'd go take the subway to visit people, and then the next they'd go back home.

From the very first day the city had been disgusting to Jimmy. He had expected to find luxury, people rich beyond belief, beautiful buildings—he'd known so little about the world, had seen nothing, traveled nowhere—and then all he found was ghetto, street gangs, garbage piled up, dilapidation all around. Years later his sister Joyce would say that leaving home was the best thing she'd ever done; Jimmy would insist it was the *worst* move he'd ever made, abandoning the frying pan for the fire.

After he got Daisy and Tonesha up there with him, he realized immediately that Jersey was no place to raise a child, that the right thing to do would be to give it all up and head for home. Then they had another daughter, Zandra, and with her birth he felt more than ever that the family didn't belong in Newark, wouldn't ever belong, had no business being there. He didn't do it, but he knew that what he needed to do was bring his girls back home.

Then came the 1967 riots, which cost him his job and trapped the whole family in their apartment while the city burned down all around them. For almost a week, twenty-four hours a day, the gunfire never stopped. Armored National Guard vehicles rumbled up and down the streets, and soldiers with machine guns manned checkpoints on street corners. The whole time, while Jimmy tried to keep his wife and girls safe, away from the windows, he dreamed of home.

In the years since he has reached the conclusion that, without a doubt, beyond any shadow of a sliver of a doubt, right then and there he should have packed up and moved back to Carolina. But he didn't. And as had always been the case except during recessions, he was able to find a new job without much trouble. Daisy also found steady work, in a factory that produced pillows and bedding. The lint in the air at work was bad for her asthma, but the pay was so good she decided to stick it out.

They had a third baby, a third daughter. Four days after she was born, when mother and baby were scheduled to come home from the hospital, Daisy's asthma flared up, and the doctors said they wanted to keep her in the hospital for a few extra days. After another week and still no improvement, Jimmy wound up checking baby Jatoya out of the hospital without Daisy. Somehow, in a blur of anxious days and nights, he managed to take care of the two little girls and their newborn sister and also visit Daisy every day and also hold on to his job. Daisy recovered slowly, and then when he finally was able to bring her home, he had to take her right back again, this time for pneumonia. The infection settled into her chest chronically, and every time it seemed she was finally shaking it off, she'd be right back in the hospital again, worse than ever.

At first Jimmy worried about whether Daisy would ever be able to get back to work. After a while, however, he was ready to settle for simply getting her out of the hospital and back to their apartment, where he could take care of everybody. There was another difficulty, too: that same year the construction industry began reacting to hints of a coming economic slowdown, and Jimmy, because of all the leave time he'd used up during Daisy's illness, was among the first people laid off. In other recessions he had managed to muddle through till building picked back up again, but in other recessions he hadn't had to take care of an invalid wife and three growing girls.

The savings account he and Daisy had been accumulating toward a place of their own back home shrank down to nothing. With his money gone, Jimmy's thoughts of home churned his stomach endlessly. More than ever he yearned to be around the homefolks, and more than ever he could use their help. But it was just too shameful to bear, the thought of going home without a dime, with his whole life in disarray. He took everybody home to visit, but they went back north again, to stick it out in Jersey. Later he concluded that he'd just been too damn stubborn, too thickheaded with pride: *All those years, the best part of living, the only good part of living, was coming home.*

Construction picked back up, and he found work. Daisy didn't recover fully, but she did do well enough to stay out of the hospital for weeks and eventually months at a time. She regained enough strength to mind the baby while Jimmy was at work and the big girls were at school. He had to do the shopping and the cooking and the cleaning, but she did what she could, sometimes more than he thought she should.

When Jatoya was three years old, she overheard her parents talking about an upcoming family reunion. *What are they talking about?* she asked her sister. *Where is down south?*

Where is down south? Jimmy gulped.

After all his years in Jersey, working good jobs, nursing his wife, raising his girls, trying to keep everybody safe and happy, it had all come to nothing. The landlord had let their apartment building decay until it was a filthy firetrap. At his daughters' school the children seemed to learn less and less each year as the building disintegrated and teachers got laid off and the crime in the neighborhood spilled into the class-rooms from the streets. Drugs were sold openly on his block, and nearby buildings that had been gutted during the riots were now collapsing or sheltering drug addicts and thugs. The streets were so dangerous he wouldn't dream of allowing his little girls out to play. Daisy's health was gone, and his was going. The diabetes that ran in his family had started to take its toll on his body.

He opened another savings account and put money aside every week, letting the bills go when he had to. A year later he moved the family back to Burdy's Bend, into a trailer on land he paid cash for.

They hadn't been home for a week before Daisy was in the hospital again. If only he could have brought her home years earlier, when she could have enjoyed life! When Jimmy got back to the trailer after driving Daisy to the hospital forty miles away, he learned that Miss Pearl had taken his two younger daughters over to her place. Things were coming full circle: she was keeping his children just as she had once kept him and Joyce.

For six months Daisy was desperately sick, rarely able to leave the hospital. The longest stretch she spent at home in their new trailer was nine days. At the end of those nine days, when Jimmy was getting into bed that night, he didn't like the sound of her breathing and decided he would have to take her to the hospital once again. She died before they got there.

She was thirty-three years old. Their daughters were fourteen, nine, and five.

*I never should have gone to Jersey, never should have gone. What did I
accomplish on the highway up there? Not much, I'm telling you. I say that
even though I can see now, bringing my kids back, that things were much
better here back when we were coming up. Back then, on Sundays, everyone
would get in the road and walk to Sunday school. This is something we had
to do every Sunday, but now they just don't do it. Not unless there is a
death in the family. We had no choices, just chores. They don't want to do
anything now.*

*I had to do everything: milk the cows, put out the cows, get them in the
afternoon, bring in the wood, pick up chips. We went to the spring to bring
water. Nowadays that's nasty water in the spring. You wouldn't dare drink
it. But back then we hauled it and drank it, washed in it. Everybody had
responsibilities. Summers, we chopped cotton, pulled up weeds, pulled up
cockleburs out of the cotton, and we topped tobacco. At night we would read
the Bible storybooks and play games. We had a lot to occupy our time. Weekends we would play ball at the baseball diamond back of the Jaguar Social
Club. Kids don't really have anything to do now.*

*I tell people to think twice about coming back, because it's hard. Maybe
if you're old or retired, but if you got to look for work, it's terrible. I was
a night guard at one of the plants, did that for four years, but, of course,
there's no work for stonemasons here, nothing like that. When I first moved
back, things were tough, I'm telling you—because of my wife and all. But
people came to my side. And I'm glad I came back. It is better for me to
raise my children here than in the city. Much better.*

*The only thing is, I wish my father had been down here to know his
grandchildren. I'm still hoping maybe I can fix up a place for him, but his
health and all, I just don't know. His kidneys are going, his eyes—it's the
diabetes, same as what I've got. Joyce and I went up to New York to see*

him last summer, when he was in the hospital for the circulation in his leg.
I don't imagine I'll be traveling up there much anymore. But he did come
down here in November, when I had my operation.

Jimmy's operation back in November had been to amputate his left leg. Since then, of course, he has been unable to
work. Tonesha, his oldest daughter, lives at home with her
father while she goes to junior college, and she takes good
care of him. Pearl has sent her son-in-law, Eula's husband Al,
to make measurements and draw up plans for a wheelchair
ramp to replace the trailer's steep front stairs; a stack of lumber has been accumulating, almost enough now to get the
project going. Pearl checks in on Jimmy at least once a day.
Each time, as soon as Pearl leaves, Joyce lets herself into the
trailer to check up on Pearl's checking up on her brother.

Both Jimmy and Joyce set forth as young adults to fulfill family roles that had been modeled for them when they were
growing up. Jimmy had a clear idea of how to be a good husband and father: like his own father and Uncle Sam, he
renounced the pleasures of home and headed north to toil
and support the homefolks. Joyce clung to dreams of life as
a good wife and mother: she sought a marriage like her Aunt
Pearl's, grounded in trust and faith and a home where children feel safe and warm. For varying reasons of character and
circumstance, neither Jimmy nor Joyce was able to follow the
paths they anticipated; perhaps few people are fully able to
do so anywhere, in any circumstances. But they knew what
they wanted in a family, and what a family could expect from
them.

A certain strength ensues from such a family sense, the

best term for which might be the one so often co-opted nowadays for superficial cant celebrating a long list of old-fashioned family virtues: respect for elders, sacrifice for others, long-term commitment, self-restraint, discipline for children, and so on. It is widely assumed that some families have all this and some are lacking it. To the extent that such definitions of family values are valid, it is obvious that Jimmy and Joyce are among the blessed: they have a strong family, long led by rugged role models, still peopled by men and women they can rely on.

Family life is a resource, sometimes the only readily available resource that poor people can turn to in times of trouble. Turning to your family is no small matter, however, for most of us: we feel a certain shame and fear a certain indebtedness. It is often a course of last resort, and even then it does not always solve problems. For example, spreading scarce resources even thinner throughout a large, poor family is no solution to the problem of poverty; it may help people get through tough times, but it does not lift them into economic security. And while the most sentimental among us might argue otherwise, if the cupboard is just flat-out bare, a dose of family values will not put bread on the table. Families can be battered into oblivion.

Jimmy and Joyce's family might well have gone under. Their mother's untimely death could have cast a dozen children to the winds of fate. Their father's migration could have frayed family bonds and deprived the children of any glimmer of fatherly love. The grinding poverty that Pearl and Samuel never escaped, the pressures of feeding child after child after child, the daily hardships of backcountry sharecropping life, the tragic accidents, the recurring illnesses, the disappointments, the disputes—under any of these burdens, not to mention under the spine-cracking weight of all of them together, many a family would collapse.

Neither Jimmy nor Joyce ever wanted to be a burden. They meant to live out on their own, worked hard for many years, and even after returning home kept struggling to remain independent. But both of them now, in different ways, are family burdens, forever needing money and basic personal care, consuming the energy and trying the patience of people around them, helplessly consuming a dozen varieties of assistance. Families are strained by such burdens, as any parent of young children has observed. When the ones needing support are adults or putative adults, whether the cause of their dependency is irresponsibility or old age or pure bad fortune, most families cannot meet the challenge without regrouping and calling out the reserves.

Who are the reserves? Many of us have been pressed into service or have anticipated situations in which we might be called upon for help. Rich people can sometimes buy their way out of the family draft by hiring help of various kinds; poor people must work as their own best help. Many of us, rich and poor, bitterly resent being asked to defer our own dreams, interrupt our own lives, forget about our own plans, so we might attend, on a permanent or long-term basis, to somebody else's needs.

But who in particular will be expected to drop everything and help out in each particular situation? Families negotiate; personal agendas are weighed against the demands of the hour. Money is almost always a factor, and in families like the

Bishops, geography obviously plays a crucial role. Jimmy's twenty-year-old daughter has assumed major responsibility for his daily care, but he is wondering how long she will be willing to serve. After she finishes school, won't she want a good job somewhere? Will she marry someone who wants to move away, or have so many children of her own that she no longer has time for her invalid father? And what if she, too, becomes a diabetic? Jimmy has watched how the disease weakened his father over the years, and he anticipates that his own health will continue to deteriorate, that he will become more and more dependent on other people. Who will he call on after Tonesha has helped as much as she can help?

Joyce, too, is anticipating such a day. She herself would like to be the one who is designated to care for Jimmy. Of course, it would be a cold day in hell before Pearl ever allowed such an arrangement, but Joyce is convinced she's the ideal person to look after her brother, if only he would trust her, give her a chance to prove what she could do. She has tried to mother his daughters, to help fill in for Daisy. She sees herself as her brother's faithful keeper—and he sees himself as his sister's very reluctant keeper, as someone who goes to endless trouble and puts up with endless aggravation to try to protect her from *her own fool self.* But even people who cannot control their own fates may need to take care of other people.

Pearl has spent fifty years taking care of children. Sometimes she has volunteered eagerly. For example, when her sister Opal had a baby out of wedlock years ago and wanted to leave town to get away from the baby's worthless father, Pearl was thrilled: she could keep the darling little girl, give Opal the fresh start she needed, and have a playmate for her own Eula. The baby was named Darlene, but from the start they called her Sissy; Eula and Sissy are still as close as any sisters.

Looking back on it all, she explains, speaking slowly and carefully, considering everything, the good and the bad, if she had it all to do over again. . . . No, she wouldn't do it again. In particular, she wouldn't keep the grandchildren.

Don't get me wrong, but I feel if I had let them live with their parents, they would be closer to them than they are. They love their parents, but they're not close to them like they should be. Every summer, when we would send them up north and they'd stay with their parents for two weeks, three weeks, before school opened, the whole time they're gone, they're calling me on the phone every day, "Ma, what you doing?" Now, that don't make no sense, them calling me every day. I'm not complaining, but look like to me they think more of me than they do their parents. I don't think that's right.

I raised my daughter Shirley's two children—they were the first grand-children I took in. She couldn't find a babysitter in New York, and Samuel said, "Well then, just bring the babies home." And now Shirley is raising her cousin's child, and her own two are still in my house, nearly grown. I raised two of Verlene's children, and also Sammy, Eula's first child, and then her second child, Edward, I had him since he was two. The children I keep don't seem to be thinking of their parents like they ought to—they're thinking of me. I'm not complaining, but it's not how it ought to be.

And now my daughters have it all over again.

Eula's nephew Andre is playing with socks in the laundry basket at her feet while she hangs out the clothes. She says she took him because Pearl has already done her part.

But there's another side to that, she insists. For Pearl, all the child-keeping is starting to pay off.

All of the children and grandchildren who are working contribute to Miss Pearl's purse. Every Friday the two oldest grandchildren come home from their jobs and give Pearl thirty dollars. My brother next door brings some of his wages home to his mother. So did Jimmy when he was working. I think he still gives her something from his disability.

And you multiply that by New Jersey, New York City, the Bronx, D.C. And the ones in the service—Germany, New Mexico. And the ones in Texas, Chicago. The one in Baltimore. They all remember a little something for her purse.

Some of the contributions to Miss Pearl's purse over the years could be considered child support payments: absent parents sending money home from their jobs up north. But other contributions, especially in recent years, are quite different in character: people who were raised by Miss Pearl are remembering her, trying to show her their gratitude, helping her out, trying to do the right thing.

Contributing to Miss Pearl's purse, like taking in a child or caring for an invalid, could be called kinwork. In every family, kinwork is redistributed from time to time in response to death, illness, the birth of a child, the loss of a job. Interdependencies are shuffled back and forth across generations— and also across the American landscape as migration in particular affects what kind of aid people can offer their families and what kind of help they might need in return.

Every family has its renegades who reject their kinwork assignments, forget Miss Pearl's purse, play havoc with family expectations, and create uncontrollable drains on family resources. Every family has its soft touches who drop everything and run to help at the first hint of a distress signal. But most people place a high value on their personal priorities as well as on their families' claims to their time and hard-earned money; families often find they have to rely on power as well as sentiment to ensure that onerous assignments are fulfilled. People do try to incorporate kinwork, current and anticipated, into their life's plans, but personal clockwork seldom meshes neatly with overall family history. Some people find themselves summoned for kinwork too early, before they have had a chance to tend to their education, their career, the needs of their children. Responding to the family's exigency may jeopardize all the dreams of a lifetime, and even mature and loving individuals may come forward only reluctantly.

When timing is a problem, when substantial sacrifice is required, when a family is too poor to buy services that might mitigate the burden, when no individual seems well suited to a particular task, family ingenuity as well as commitment can be tested. The families returning to Burdy's Bend, New Jericho, Chowan Springs, and Rosedale—along with the families receiving them there—are devising new patterns of assigning kinwork, writing new scripts for old family values.

5

Clyde's Dilemma

The men and women in New York and other cities who are keeping an eye on goings-on in places like Rosedale and Burdy's Bend often find that one particular turn of events back home stands out as painfully salient: the grandparents and other relatives who raised them are aging, ailing, and dying. No one is ready when parents or grandparents can no longer take care of themselves, even if preparations have been laid. Not everyone responds by quitting work and moving right back home. But poverty limits choices, and cultural values fashion expectations, until returning to take care of an aging relative may seem like the only thing to do. Many people regard a call for such help as their most immediate call to home. Once they are resettled back home, people often decide to stay.

Clyde's "letter" is a research construct designed to elicit discussion of tensions between personal agendas and family pressures. Like the half-dozen respondents quoted here, the vast majority of people who spoke with me about Clyde's dilemma recounted personal experience caring for older family members. In some families a summons to provide such care was directly linked to an individual's decision to move back home, and in other families it was part of the background of expectations that molded a whole series of moves and decisions.

Dear Abby,

I am an unmarried man who lives in Washington, D.C. I work part-time as a security guard. My parents live back home in Rosedale, which is a small town out in the country, about 250 miles south of D.C. My mother has been bedridden for a couple of years, and my father has sugar and recently lost a leg, so he can't take care of her anymore. My two sisters in New Jersey have both had a turn taking care of them and hope to move back home eventually, but right now the older one has a good job and the younger one just got married. Both of my sisters think I am the one who should go back home and take care of my parents. What do you think I should do?

—Clyde

Ralph, age 33:

R: I may not be answering the question that you want me to answer, but I will tell you what I did when I was working at a department store in Philly and my sister was there with me teaching. My grandfather and mother were still alive, and I went home for a vacation. My mother was in the hospital, and they couldn't find nobody to be with my grandfather. I went back up and asked for a leave of absence, but they didn't grant it to me, so I just gave my job up and came home. My mother came home from the hospital and died four months later. I stayed on to take care of my grandfather. He seemed more like my father—I've never known my father. I was still north when my grandmother died. It just don't seem real that she's gone. I won't go back north now.

   But for Clyde . . . in my opinion, I think it should be a lady.

I: Why do you think it should be a lady?

R: Well, it could be either way.

I: I was wondering why you felt it should be a woman?

R: The lady is bedridden. Maybe she don't want no man to be taking care of her in that position. You taping that?

I: Yeah. Nobody knows who it is I'm talking to.

R: Okay. I just feel like it should be a woman. That's my opinion. But I do know of a case . . . this lady is dead and gone. She has been dead about two years. There was nobody at home but her husband and her son. The father, when she had to use the pot, he helped her. When she needed to be turned over in bed, he did it. The father had a stroke. He couldn't do all these things, and his son took over. He bathed her, too.

When my grandfather needed that kind of care, I pulled the shade. I ain't seen nothing. I bathed him.

I: Did you feel uncomfortable about bathing him?

R: I ain't never done anything like that before. I just pulled the shade, so I wouldn't see nothing. Later on I got used to it. But if it's a woman . . . if possible, a lady should do it.

Beatrice, age 43:

B: I think Clyde should go home.

I: Why do you think so?

B: He's only working part-time in the big city. He would probably survive just as well in the country doing odd jobs, and then he could help his mother and father. Then again, they may have some work on the farm for him, ten or twelve head of cattle.

I: I don't think his family had land, just a house.

B: From just a purely moral thing then, I think he should come home. He could make arrangements, find county and state services available to an invalid. When my father was sick, my mother was able to take care of his day-to-day existence, just like I did with my mother. My sister and I worked out time periods to go home. That's before we moved back from Philly. My mother had a brief illness, but still we had to handle it, so we traded off.

Louis, age 37:

L: I don't see where Clyde has much of an alternative. That is my opinion. Of course, I have a family situation like that. All of my older brothers and sisters were married and had their own families—one was in school, another just started teaching. I was single and on my own. My daddy had been farming all his life. When he passed, there were about eight children underage. My mother had the farm, but there wasn't nobody left to take over. All the older kids jumped on me to come back and help Mom. I was soft enough to fall for it, and I never regretted it. I was kind of getting attached to the city life, so to speak, in Jersey back then, but I came down and farmed with my brother before he went to Vietnam.

I: You farmed? The city boy farmed?

L: Yeah, yeah. I was raised on the farm. I know all about it. I stayed and helped for five years. As wild as I was, I did what I was supposed to do. I just did it.

When I got married, I bought me a car and took off. I stayed away for ten years and came back with my wife just three years ago. My sister who taught school, she lives over across the road from my place. And then my brother who was in Vietnam built his house over behind my place.

Clayton, age 42:

C: By me being a man, I got no business even bathing a daughter no more after three years old. And I don't think the mama would want her son bathing her.

I: Why do you think that?

C: Is she confined to a bed? That mean she has got to be bathed and everything. They are some sorry daughters if the son have to do it. And how those daughters going to feel if their mama don't live?

In a family with three or more children, out of those offspring you usually have one who wants to come back and oversee the home and the finances. Since Clyde's the only male in the family, and his sisters decided to stay in D.C., Clyde is next in line in terms of manly responsibilities. In my opinion, if Clyde really love his mama and she wants him to come home, I say, yeah, don't let her end up in a rest home somewhere. You know, a lot of people love a dollar, and they tend to love a dollar better than they love human beings. It's up to the individual.

I: What about if it were you?

C: If it were me instead of Clyde? Oh Lord. I guess I would come home and take care of her. Somebody has to do it. You wouldn't want to put them in a nursing home. I think families should take care of families. Getting old is no disgrace. It's a cycle. They had to feed us and wipe our butt. We just do the same for them. That's the way I feel about it.

Marlene, age 35:

M: I think Clyde should make arrangements for somebody to stay with his mother or have her placed in a nursing home. That way, it won't impose so many hardships and disrupt their children's lives. They won't have to give up their jobs. All three could chip in to pay for help. They need to sit down and talk this thing over. Clyde may be elected to do what his sisters profit from. It is not going to be an easy decision for any of them. But to put the mother in a nursing home, they better have a whole lot of money, and if they have any property, it is all going to the nursing home. So in the end they may lose their land. And Social Services is not going to provide much help.

They should have looked down the road and seen this situation coming. To draw full benefits from your government supplements, you can't own any property. The property should have been transferred a long time ago, with the parents having lifetime rights.

I: Do you think people do that ordinarily?

M: Oh yeah. They foresee a situation. Putting things like that off worsens the situation. Now they are at a point that they really can't afford a nursing home or someone to stay twenty-four hours a day, seven days a week. A nursing home! J. Paul Getty couldn't afford one now, and they don't get the care they should get. They are understaffed. It's a lot to think about.

We made the same mistake with our Aunt Iola, my mother's sister. She was getting around, and one day she just went out—her legs gave way—and we took her to the hospital. They did a CAT scan and told us she had a brain tumor on the base of her brain. The tumor had gone down her spine and was inoperable.

If we had been on the ball, we would have transferred all of Aunt Iola's assets over to us. At the hospital they said she had to go directly to a nursing facility. We should take everything out of her name and then apply for Medicaid. I went to apply for her and gave them all the information that I knew. They checked on every aspect of her business. "What did she write the $1,000

check to her brother for?" "Does she own her own home?"
I told them she gave the home to me. "When did she give
the home to you?"

I: You know a lot about these issues now!

M: You came to the right person. I think and talk to people
about planning, especially if they have a house or land.
We lost everything. Rich folks know that this thing has
to be done in degrees. I've been thinking about this a lot.
There's information we don't have that we need to know
about property. And we all have such complicated feelings about nursing homes.

I: What are yours?

M: One day a neighbor came over to visit and told my dad
that his oldest friend had been put in a nursing home
because his wife couldn't take care of him. This guy came
over and told Dad that. It really upset my father—I
mean, for about four days afterwards. They were good
friends, but what was running through his mind was if
we were going to put *him* in a nursing home. It upset him
to the point that he thought he would be next. It upset
him so bad that he almost had another heart attack. So
that's how I feel.

   Of course, we didn't put him anywhere. When my
father was sick, we rotated the care between the three of
us. We were all back here by that time. He didn't have to
go to a nursing home.

Elsie, age 45:

E: It has come with our age group that we face a season of
illness and then death with our parents. We have been

struck within our family. We lost four relatives in the last four months. A cousin of mine, an older cousin, was funeralized two weeks ago.

Clyde has been put in a pretty awful situation. I don't think they should put the load on one person. He is entitled to his life, too. It's going to be an extreme sacrifice for him, quitting his job. All three of them should chip in and help. It is a family situation. They should all come down here and make decisions together. His sisters should come help so that the responsibility is not all dumped on Clyde.

I: If Clyde says no, he is within his rights to do so?

E: Certainly he is. It seems like they are imposing on him because he is single. He is a child like all the rest of them. But Clyde should do his part—it is still his parents. If the sisters absolutely won't come back, then he should come home. That is just my opinion. I think family is the most important sacrifice that we all should make.

Social Services doesn't pay children to take care of parents, and these days rest homes are extremely dangerous. I don't know Clyde's income, but I don't think he could afford a convalescent home. As a rule, blacks do not put their parents in a rest home. They try everything else that's possible—a rest home is the last resort.

I: How close to home does this come to your own life?

E: Look at my grandma. She can't cook, can't use the bathroom, can't bathe herself, but we all chip in and make sure that she is taken care of. It is very gratifying for us to do that. Luckily, my stepfather is there, so we don't have to stay the night.

When it gets a little rough for me, I have my niece to go in the morning to give her a bath and breakfast. I wash her clothes and take her meals and snacks and check on her. It is not so hard if somebody helps. I'm lucky to have my girls home with me. They help out. I got to be at work at 2:00 P.M., and I get off at 11:00 P.M. My older daughter takes over if I'm tired and gives Grandma a sponge bath, puts her gown on, turns her bed back, gives her dinner. It's not solely my responsibility. I am very well blessed.

It's going to be a big job for Clyde. He can't bathe her. What man wants to give his mama a bath? It's time-consuming when someone is bedridden. It is like going back to childhood. They don't want to cooperate with you; they still want their individualism. That is when it gets hard. It is just overwhelming. I can't get away weekends.

I: You are sort of held a prisoner to your own responsibilities.

E: My girls are young, I can't depend on them. And I want my girls to have their own lives to live. I am grateful they are helping me, but I am not going to saddle them with Ma. But it feels like it is all on my shoulders.

I keep Grandma's house up. I have to see the porch is fixed, the bathroom, make hot water. My grandma gets $187 per month Social Security. What can you do with that little money? Her diapers, underpads, for two weeks cost $22.95. Then she has medication and three meals a day. I want them to eat three balanced meals a day.

I: You mean you have the financial responsibility?

E: Sure I do, every penny, every dime. I don't have a sister or brother to walk up to me and say, "Honey, here's $20."

Well, my mother sends us some, but not much, and my husband helps.

I: Your grandmother is very fortunate.

E: She is one of the luckiest ladies. . . . She is very lucky. So that's my answer to your question.

Carla, age 22:

C: What should Clyde do? I guess . . . I don't know really. What I want to say is, he should go on home, but I keep thinking of my next-door neighbor.

I: Your neighbor?

C: Wilma Hines, do you know her?

I: I'm not sure.

C: Well, she did exactly what you ought to do. In fact, I'd say she went the extra mile. And she wasn't ready to come back yet either. But I'm not so sure it's working out.

I: What do you mean, about not working out?

C: You really need to talk to her directly. She's somebody who's just tried as hard as a person can try, and even so . . . just go talk to her.

Wilma Hines, age 42:

My husband got into gambling in Jersey. We were only nineteen, but I could see it was leading nowhere. After two years he was still at it, so we separated. I came back home with my girls for a short time but left again. I had to get away from here to support them. I would have taken anything so long as I was working back home and we could be together, but there were no jobs. I chose Philly because my mother was there.

I went right to work the second day after I arrived. I didn't like assembly-line work—sticking pins in dolls' heads to make them stand stiff, it drove me crazy. But it was work. Eventually I got a different job, at a drugstore, then at another factory, and later at the phone company. I was fortunate enough to get a job at the Vet—the VA hospital—teaching people how to walk with prosthesis. They trained me. For ten years I worked nights at the phone company—I kept that job—and days at the Vet hospital, and I was able to send money home every week.

I hated to leave my babies when I first left. It was a terrible struggle for me, especially since it was a repeat of my own experiences. I remembered when I was a child wanting so badly to move to the city to be where my mother was. I knew I couldn't have my two girls with me in Philly, working around the clock as I was, but I would be so happy to wake up and be with them. I went to see them every three months; I never stayed away from them more than three months at a time. I kept the road hot. It was several years before I was able to come back and get them. They were eleven and twelve.

My mother is still in Philly, and she was a blessing to me up there, not only giving moral support, phone calls and all, but financial support, too. A couple of times, when I needed money—not small money—it came. Either one of us had, and the other one didn't, or vice versa; there has never been a time when both of us didn't have. Some of the time when I needed her help, we lived together. It didn't matter to my daughters which of us cared for them. They didn't cry for their mommy when they were with her. They were lucky. That's the way we are, a family bunch of folks.

Both of my girls stayed with me until my half-sister Tilly got sick. My girls moved in with her in Baltimore for almost two years to help out with her children. After she died, all her children and my girls came to me for a while, but then her children wanted to go back south. My half-sister who died . . . I am an only child, I am, but it's complicated. My real mother's sister is still living in Baltimore. She's the one that gave birth to me. The one I call my real mother is her sister, the one that took me and raised me since I was two months old. That's mother to me.

My younger daughter is still in Philly. She stayed there to be near my mother when I had to come back. To be honest, I wasn't ready to come back when I did around the latter part of 1978, but I am an only child, and my grandparents are elderly, and they needed somebody to be with them. I was ready to leave the rat race. I was tired. But I wasn't ready to leave, because I wanted to build a house back home for my parents. I didn't care how I got the money, as long as it was legal, as long as I was working for it, two jobs, whatever. But I had no choice but to leave.

What was so hard when I came back was trying to help my grandfather. In Philly I was working at a hospital with wounded Vietnam vets. I could do anything with them. A single amputee or a double amputee, when they got their prosthesis, I could, with the help of God Almighty, teach them how to walk. If there was a partial paralysis, I could teach them to eat with shaking hands. Eventually I could teach them how to bring their hand directly to their mouth. I could see that I was doing something. In the two and half years that I have been back working with my grandfather, I don't see any results. I'm doing what I have been taught to do, and he doesn't respond, doesn't even try. I hate it.

I had started buying my land while I was working in Philly and got it paid for before I came home. When I got back, I had to find a job, because I wanted to build a house. My mind went to nursing assistant, because of my experience, but I couldn't find anything. I heard that they were going to try out some women at the sawmill, and heck, if they're going to pay in dollars, I would try it. Working there was disgusting. But the sawmill was getting the house built. After a few months I got a job at a nursing home. Nursing homes are filthy, too, and the aides get the dirty end of the stick. You bathe the patients, you change the beds, you empty the pot. The aides know the patients more than the RNs or doctors do, but we didn't get the respect or money we deserved. People would say, "You're not a nurse." I had to overcome the part of being looked down upon for being an aide. I would have preferred being called a nurse's assistant.

I know what I am doing is important, and that I am one of the best aides in the world. No matter. Nothing that I can do that I have learned in my training helps me with my papa. When he lost his eyesight, I should have been able to teach him how to go all over the house, how to feed himself through his blindness. It worked with everybody else I taught, but it won't work for him. People tell me it's because he's my grandfather and he sees me as his child giving him orders. It's okay for me to clean the filth off him, but don't teach him how to do anything. It blows my mind. It hurts, because I know I could, but I can't with him. Papa has two good legs, and I can't teach him how to walk.

I got knocked down by it, but then I look on the inside of me and know it is still there. But it doesn't work with him, even though it has worked with everyone else. That hurts me to tears. But there is a lesson in it: there's things you can't do. You can't do everything.

When I first got back, I was determined that, if somebody else could live in a decent house, then I could get my parents out of the house they were in and put them in a decent house. I was determined to give them the best of everything that I could give them.

With the money I was earning, I turned over the deeds to FmHA and got the house started. But I never knew how long I was going to be on this or that job. I felt more vulnerable than any other time in my life—my income for the house depended upon my employers. For the first time in my life, after being a hard worker but an honest worker on the job in Philly, I learned to keep my mouth shut or have the right things come out of it to my white boss. I also was dealing with a corrupt contractor. I paid for material that I could see being stolen away. You can't stay and watch every brick, every nail. At one point I had to get a lawyer to intervene. I would go to work at Mrs. Smith's so depressed. It is a headache for a woman to build a house by herself, because people walk all over you.

My mother lived in the house for two years before she died in 1982. My father has been bedridden for the past two years. Because of that, I'm not working. I just can't. There have been days when I wanted to shove Papa into a rest home, but I promised him I never would as long as I was breathing.

6

Holding Hands

Holding Hands wasn't the first women's service organization in Chestnut County. By the time of its official charter in December 1981, there were already two other such groups: the Chestnut Education Circle, which a woman named Menola Rountree had started back in the 1950s to sponsor an annual beauty walk and raise money for college and trade-school scholarships, and Worldly Women, which held teen dances every month or so to bring together young people from the various churches in the county, most of which were too small for youth ministries or young people's fellowships of their own. Chestnut County was still just a little country place—in 1980 census takers had counted fewer than 1,000 people in the county seat, Chowan Springs, and just 467 in Rosedale, the next-largest town—but nonetheless, the three women behind Holding Hands believed that the time had come for another women's group, an organization that would try to tackle the problems of Chestnut County head-on, taking an approach that was literally hands-on.

The idea for Holding Hands could be traced to a back-yard barbecue in late October of 1981. But the history actually went much further back than that, as any of the women involved could explain. It went back to the painful lessons the women had begun learning in 1979, when the first of them moved home again from the Bronx. And then back behind those lessons were ways of dealing with the world that the Holding Hands women had developed in the 1960s and 1970s while working their way through school, selling Amway products and life insurance, moving to the city, raising families, running PTAs and scout troops, and working in corporate offices and government agencies. Even more fundamentally, the roots of Holding Hands had been planted back in the 1950s when the women were growing up in Chestnut County as the daughters of sharecroppers and as best, best, best friends who just knew that everything was going to work out all right.

The three little girls, Shantee, Isabella, and Collie Mae, eventually acquired the matronly names of Shantee Owens, Isabella Beasley, and Collie Mae Gamble. All of them kept in touch over the years and got together often, but two of them in particular, Isabella and Collie Mae, carried their girlhood friendship to a new level in adulthood. For many years they were living hundreds of miles apart and were thus unable to rely on one another for day-to-day companionship and conversation; instead, they each took over responsibility for managing the other's career. For example, on the day before Isabella married Rudy Beasley, she took Collie Mae, who had driven up to Newark so she could be maid of honor in the wedding, over to the Civil Service office and arranged for her to take the employment exam. After Isabella moved back home and told Collie Mae about the shameful state of day-care services in Chestnut County, Collie Mae asked around her church until she located a *gentleman* who owned an abandoned gas station and persuaded him to make it available rent-free for a model day-care center. Neither woman could imagine changing jobs or making any major decisions about her professional life without consulting the other.

Shantee kept a little more distance, preferred a little more privacy. She wasn't a loner exactly, and she certainly wasn't shy, but perhaps people were left with some such impression because of the contrast with her mother, the inimitable and irrepressible Orlonia Parks, de facto toastmistress of Chestnut County. In 1946 a Rosedale boy named Halliburton Parks had been detailed over to Powell County by the lumbering outfit he worked for, and ever since he robbed the cradle over there to bring back fifteen-year-old Orlonia as his bride, life in Chestnut County had not been the same. No church meeting, school function, civic event, or gathering of any kind was complete without a few words from Miss Orlonia. She was the one who could get everybody to sit down and hush up, and she was also the one who could get everybody on their feet and roaring for action. People remembered her words: for example, instead of repeating a conventional expression such as "between a rock and a hard place," Miss Orlonia would say something like "between a dog and a tree."

As soon as Shantee was old enough to toddle onto the stage behind her mother, Orlonia had dragged her along and pushed her forward at every occasion. Shantee couldn't help but grow up poised and comfortable in public, though she backed off from her mother's down-to-earth imagery and developed a reputation for delivering even the most off-the-cuff remarks in a formal and polished cadence. But she, too, could turn a phrase that set people to giggling. *I am here today,* she once told an audience, *because my mother suggested that it would be in my best interest, or her best interest—or perhaps what she meant was that it would be* interesting—*if I got out of the house a bit and, shall we say,* established *myself.* Sometimes, however, Shantee left her listeners with a sense that she knew more than she would tell. People who liked her said she was discreet, and people who didn't like her said she was secretive.

Collie Mae and Isabella liked her very much and suspected secret sadnesses in her life. She'd been the first of the three to leave home, back in 1967, one day after they all graduated from East Chestnut High. She had stayed up north the longest, till the summer of 1983; Collie Mae had returned two years earlier, and Isabella two years before that. Everybody knew all about the fancy life she'd led up in New York. Orlonia left no one in the dark about how Shantee had gone to college and taught school for a while and then gone to work for a company that ran workshops in school districts all over the country, training teachers in the use of new curricular materials. *Shantee rides an airplane to work every day,* Miss Orlonia told Chestnut County. *She teaches teachers how to teach.*

Shantee's high school boyfriend, Anthony Owens, had sulked and pined after she left. He hadn't promised to wait for her—in fact, he'd threatened *not* to wait for her—but when she didn't come home and didn't come home, he finally moved up north himself to live with his uncle in the Bronx. Shantee was going to school at the time and claimed to be much too busy for a social life, so the only way Anthony could think of to get to see her was to enroll in school himself, signing up for the same classes she was taking. He eventually became a parole officer in Harlem, and they were married in 1972. The apartment they moved into was up on the thirty-fifth floor and had shag carpeting on the floor and track lighting in the ceiling. They had two black cocker spaniels. They never had children.

Isabella, meanwhile, stayed home while she attended a community college down near the coast, about an hour's drive from Chowan Springs. She got an associate's degree and then moved in with her sister in Newark, where she met a boy from home, Rudy Beasley, who was just back from Vietnam. Their wedding was Chestnut County's social event of the year, though it took place in Newark; half the county attended. Rudy went into the home remodeling business with his brothers, and Isabella worked for a state agency that administered federal funds for Head Start and Title XX day-care programs. They eventually had two daughters, who worried Isabella sick all day every day, especially when they became teenagers. Newark was no place to raise children.

Collie Mae had the hardest time leaving home. She had been sent up north for three years back when she was in junior high school and her mother was dying of cancer; once the family was reassembled at home on their farm near Chowan Springs, she felt personally responsible for ensuring that things went smoothly. She lived with her father and her four little sisters and her father's mother, and though she was trying to take a full-time course load at a traditionally black teachers' college sixty-five miles from the farm, she also helped her grandmother with the cooking and the ironing and the washing, and she helped her father with farm chores and kept the books for him, and she helped her sisters with their schoolwork, and she worked part-time as a maid at a motel on the highway. When her grandmother fell ill, she took over all the cooking and ironing and washing, and she killed hogs, plucked chickens, put up vegetables for winter, nursed her grandmother, took over the main responsibility for raising her little sisters—and never stopped going to school. Some semesters she had to reduce her course load, but she never once dropped out.

Her grandmother died when Collie Mae was twenty-one and about halfway finished with her degree in business administration. After the funeral, every time she thought about her grandmother, she couldn't stop herself from also thinking about her mother; she was walking in the shadow of the valley of death, fearful and uncomforted. To keep herself from dwelling on her losses, she increased her course load at school to twenty-one semester hours, well above the full-time level, and she increased her work week at the motel to forty hours, sometimes more. Her housework and farmwork didn't

really let up, but it only took her one more year and two summer sessions to become a college graduate.

She still felt needed at home, so she framed her diploma
and hung it on the wall over the living room sofa, and she
kept her job as a motel maid and tried to figure out what she
could do with her life. The idea of applying for a fancy professional job seemed unpromising; hardly ever did jobs of
that sort come open in Chestnut County, but even if an
opening did come up, everybody knew Collie Mae as a farm
girl who cleaned motel rooms. Who would believe she'd
turned herself into someone at a whole different level?

Finally, Isabella came back home and talked some sense
into her. *You are one stubborn girl,* she said. *Look at how you went to
school. You never gave up, you kept on fighting against the odds, you worked
twenty-five hours a day, you wouldn't take no for an answer. Those are
advantages—they're your strengths in life. You're persistent. What you need
is a job selling something.*

So Collie Mae signed up with an insurance company that
offered accident and burial policies for poor people. The
policies cost twenty-five dollars and stayed in effect for six
months, so twice a year she revisited her old customers to try
to collect premiums. In between she and the other salespeople canvassed county by county, walking every dirt road,
visiting every shack. They started off each morning with pep
rallies to psych themselves up, and they practiced setting
daily performance goals: how many contacts, how many successful closings. From the very first day Collie Mae was the
top trainee. No matter how high she set her daily goals, she
routinely exceeded them, and none of the other salespeople
came close to her performance. She completed the most sales

visits, earned the most in commissions, and won trophies from the company.

Her base salary was five hundred dollars a month. When her sales performance exceeded a certain quota, she earned commissions on top of the base, but when people signed up for a policy and then didn't pay, the missing premiums would be deducted from her salary. Collie Mae was surprised at first by how many customers didn't pay; it was an everyday thing for people to act as though they had the money when they really didn't. She started looking more closely at the conditions in which people were living, and what she saw turned her stomach.

I saw people living worse off than I ever imagined, and I had always thought my family was poor. I knocked on the door of one house and found people living in a part of a house that didn't have a roof! They were living in the one good room in an abandoned house that was all caved in. They used a car battery to charge their refrigerator. There was no running water. They had to tote water from way down the road. I'd say it was well over a mile to this one gas station that would let them take water. And, of course, they had no car. And they paid forty dollars a month for rent!

These folks didn't have any job, no job skills, and they had no car. Even if they got a job, how would they get to work? Who would take care of their kids? Their room was freezing cold in the winter. Some people have welfare and food stamps, but one family I met, they didn't even know to go get it. Some people don't go. There's some that can't get into town to get to the welfare office. And then there's some families that just don't want it. They'd rather be cold and hungry and do what they are doing than have somebody breathing down their backs or calling their neighbors and asking about them.

Collie Mae began to feel an urgent need to get away. Surely there was some place on earth where things were better, where she wouldn't have to live all day every day breathing in the stench of poverty and desperation. Although there was no shortage of work for her at home around the farm, her sisters were getting old enough to help out. She began taking more and more vacations—always heading to New Jersey to visit Isabella—and the family seemed to get by all right without her. The vacations began to seem absolutely necessary to save her sanity. She'd already taken and passed the state civil service exam, so the next step, the final break, was easier than she had ever dreamed: her sisters cried and her father seemed dazed, in a state of shock, but nobody told her flat out not to go. On a certain level, they understood. She took a job processing bids on government contracts in Camden, New Jersey, a town just across the Delaware River from Philadelphia.

The workload was unbelievable. For the first month she went in to work early every day and stayed late and brought huge stacks of papers home and stayed up half the night, and still she couldn't catch up. No sooner did she pick up one piece of paper than ten more appeared on her desk. No matter how hard she tried, she couldn't come close to working fast enough.

At the end of the month she figured it all out: the man who shared the cubicle with her was dumping most of his own work on her. She was trying to keep up with two people's work while he sat around sucking on peppermints and reading *True Detective* magazine. The minute she realized what was going on, she excused herself, went into the ladies' room, locked the door, and cried. Then she washed her face, figured out exactly what she should say to the man, and went back up to him and said it. That was the end of the problem.

Through her cousins in Camden, Collie Mae met a young man who also had Chestnut County roots, though he'd spent more of his life in New Jersey than he had back home. He was a journeyman electrician. They were married in 1975, and in 1976 they arranged for one of Collie Mae's sisters to come up and move in with them to help take care of their new baby, Aleisha. Camden was beginning to feel like home.

But Isabella was already plotting to leave Newark. Her daughters were entering their teenage years, and she worried about them every minute. They were supposed to walk straight home after school and call her at work the minute they got in. They had to stay in the apartment, with the door locked; they couldn't go anywhere or have anyone over while she was at work. On weekends, if they went out, they had to call when they got there, and then call again before they went anywhere else, and she always had to know exactly who they were with and what they were doing and how they were going to get there and when they would be home—and it was no way to live. The girls resented all the rules and rebelled from time to time, or snuck around behind their mother's back, covering up for each other. Isabella understood how they felt but was just plain terrified to let up on them. Even when they were at school she worried: from everything she'd heard, education was just about the last priority in some of those class-rooms.

She began investigating private schools. She and Rudy both made decent money, though in the construction indus-try he couldn't always count on having a good year. But even with two incomes, the bills got away from them sometimes. They were still making payments on Isabella's college loans, as well as trying to send money home every month and saving up for a piece of land and a house of their own. Isabella decided that the only way they could afford private school tuition would be by adding a third source of income, and when she discussed the problem with Collie Mae, she got an instant answer: she should set herself up in some kind of business.

The business she eventually chose—over Rudy's strenuous objections, which she interpreted as lack of imagination on his part—was a distributorship for a high-priced line of cleaning supplies called Diamond. They had to put in three thousand dollars up front, an investment that they could recover slowly by selling cleaning supplies or much more rapidly by bringing in new investors. But their three-thousand-dollar check had scarcely cleared the bank before the Diamond empire collapsed, and like all the other would-be "distributors" in the pyramid, Isabella and Rudy Beasley lost every dime of their money. They learned later that their three-thousand-dollar loss ranked them among the luckiest of Diamond's victims; some people lost as much as forty or fifty thousand.

But right after it happened, when they were still feeling decidedly unlucky and were floundering emotionally, desperate for someone or something to blame, Collie Mae drove up to Newark for the weekend, with little Aleisha, to try to cheer up her old friend Isabella. Sparks of marital hostility were flaring into flame in the Beasley apartment; Isabella and Rudy seemed to be going after each other with blowtorches. *I'm warning y'all, cut that out,* insisted Collie Mae. *It's gonna be all right. I know just what it is you need to do now.*

What they needed to do now was sell Amway products. The initial investment required was less than a hundred dollars.

We'd been burned once, really burned, so it was hard for me to develop a positive attitude when I first got into Amway. My husband wasn't supportive at all—he just didn't see the opportunities. It's not that he couldn't see it, he just wouldn't see it. After that first experience we'd had, his heart wasn't in it at all. But I tell people that I am an Amway lifer.

I truly believe in their philosophy. It works. The whole basis of the Amway philosophy is positive thinking, and I have learned—they have taught me, in the seminars and so forth—that everything stems from positive thinking. I could apply that attitude in my everyday life—there are always people who are going to try to psych me out, but if I can take the approach of positive thinking, it doesn't get to me. In life there are little things every day that get to people, and they wipe a lot of people out, but I just keep saying to myself, girl, keep on going. Keep on going.

I'm still in Amway. I haven't made a fortune at it. I could have, I think. I could have done very well, especially if my husband had gotten as much out of it as I have. But aside from the money, in terms of what I have learned about life, yes, absolutely, I'm an Amway lifer.

While Isabella was plunging into Amway, Rudy tried another tack. He took the girls back home for a summer vacation and used what little was left of their savings to buy a small lot at the edge of Chowan Springs. For three weeks they all camped out in a tent on their lot while he and one of his brothers, who'd already moved home to stay, poured the foundation and a concrete slab. They went back to Newark for the school year, and then the next summer they camped on the slab while Rudy framed the house. The summer after that, in 1978, they moved back home for good, camping in the house shell while Rudy did the finishing work. The girls enrolled in East Chestnut High School.

Isabella stayed on in Newark. She didn't know what to do;

at one point she was on the verge of joining the family in Carolina when she was offered a promotion at work that she just couldn't turn down. Her job was a joy: she oversaw the grant application process for Head Start and day-care funding, helped set up training programs for care providers, and visited project sites to evaluate their strengths and weaknesses. Every day she felt she was learning something new about the intricacies of government bureaucracies and community organizing efforts. She watched community organizations develop programs that grew and flourished, and she watched other organizations struggle for years and finally fail. She watched and learned and made good money and missed her family every moment.

To economize, she gave up the apartment in Newark and moved in with her sister, sleeping on the couch. Virtually every cent she earned went straight to Rudy, for plumbing fixtures, lumber, roofing shingles, electrical conduit, insulation, siding, and whatever tools he needed that he couldn't beg or borrow. Rudy and his brother were experienced builders who knew how to cut corners when they had to, but Isabella felt that watching the building process from hundreds of miles away was nerve-wracking enough without having to worry about corner-cutting. When they discussed things on the phone, she would always advise him to wait and save up until they could afford to do this or that job properly, but he would always respond that he did not need sidewalk superintendence from the sidewalks of Newark.

At one point he bought an old barn for a few dollars and spent almost a month tearing it carefully apart for the lumber. Only after he had hauled all the wood over to his lot did he look at it carefully enough to determine that termites had ruined almost all of it.

Isabella's response was to sell more Amway so she could send home more money and he could build the house faster. She rode the Greyhound bus back and forth to Chowan Springs and started selling some Amway products to friends and relatives there. Even after all her years up north, she still knew a lot of people in Chestnut County, and sales were better than she had expected. In fact, she sold so much Amway back home that she began to form a plan in her mind: maybe she could quit her job in New Jersey even before she'd found a new job in Carolina, and move back home where she belonged, with her family, relying on Amway to finish paying for the house and tide them over till she could get another real job.

In the summer of 1979, almost exactly a year behind Rudy and the girls, Isabella moved back to Chowan Springs. For the next five years she scoured Chestnut and surrounding counties for any job of any kind that she might be even remotely qualified for. But she never worked at a regular job again. Rudy's occasional construction jobs and Isabella's Amway did in fact finish the house and see the family through until she was able to bring in funds from the outside world to create steady work for herself and many dozens of other people.

Collie Mae watched enviously from New Jersey as Isabella settled herself back in at home. Ever since Aleisha's birth, she'd been paying close and nervous attention to Isabella's adventures and misadventures raising daughters up north, and even over the phone she could hear the relief in her friend's voice once the girls were safely back in Chowan Springs. Aleisha was a thriving toddler, enrolled in a Montessori preschool and happily spending weekends and evenings with her little cousins in Philadelphia. But Collie Mae was already worried about the sorts of problems that a child—a girl in particular—would have to learn to deal with growing up in a big city.

Also, the phone calls from her father begging her to return were growing more and more frequent, and more and more depressing. He always tried to sound upbeat, but she could hear undertones of stress, even desperation, in his voice. The farm was a disaster; high interest on FHA loans and a run of bad seasons were threatening to destroy a lifetime of devoted stewardship of the land. Her father was a resourceful, community-minded man; out in back of his equipment sheds, for example, he'd put up rental houses, and he'd turned an old soybean field into a baseball diamond. He didn't charge for use of the baseball field but did require all the teams to pick up paper and other litter after the games. His latest idea to save the place was to put up a trailer park out in a field where he'd once grown peanuts. *Sounds like a pretty good crop to me, growing trailers,* he told Collie Mae. *Soon as you're ready to come on back home, I believe we could raise us a right nice little crop of trailers.*

She almost felt ready to come on home. Her father seemed so lonesome, and so up against the wall. He'd had such a hard life, losing his wife and then his mother, raising five children all by himself. As the oldest of the children, Collie Mae felt by far the closest to him. And anyway, her little sisters weren't really ready yet to think about settling down. Two of them stayed in Camden with Collie Mae for a while, and then one went home to go to nursing school and the other moved in with a third sister and their aunt in Philadelphia. The youngest one had joined the army and was about to be sent to Germany. One of the ones in Philadelphia said she and her boyfriend were going to move to California as soon as he got his disability settlement from his motorcycle accident. They were kids, still eager to see the world, but as Collie Mae approached her thirtieth birthday, she was already beginning to feel old and worn down.

Her husband wasn't opposed to moving back home—as an electrician, he was sure he could find work around there somewhere—but he was loudly opposed to moving in with Collie Mae's father. *When your daddy is around me, all he sees is a new farmhand to put to work,* he complained. *I just can't be bossed around like that. I ain't cut out to be a farmboy.*

Eventually, despite his qualms, going home began to seem like the only option. They wrote a letter to one of her father's tenants, asking them to move out at their earliest convenience, which turned out to be five months later, in the spring of 1981; inexpensive housing was hard to find. They moved into the little house in back of her father's shed and got Aleisha a puppy and even a sad old spotted pony. Collie Mae's husband, anxious to make certain that her father didn't mistake him for a farmhand, dressed in a suit and tie every morning and carried an attaché case containing his résumé, which he presented to potential employers all over Chestnut and surrounding counties. Nobody hired him.

Collie Mae thought he was going about his job search all wrong.

He just looked like such a city slicker. "You don't wear fancy clothes and *hand out a résumé," I kept telling him. "At least go in your blue jeans, look like you're ready to work." People here don't want a résumé. Really, in his heart, he had become a city slicker. When he finally got a job at the meat-packing company, they put him on the floor pulling off hogs—and you know, a city guy down here, this frustrated him.*

It was real hard for him. And there was an old girlfriend, too, which is something I hadn't known about before we moved back, but it became obvi-ous. She kept showing up for this excuse and that excuse, her car would just show up in the driveway. I thought about, you know, having words with her, but it wasn't the kind of life I wanted. Finally he just stopped coming home, and we separated within about six months of moving back.

A few weeks after Collie Mae's husband left, she and her father hosted a barbecue in honor of Shantee Owens and her husband, who were back home for a long weekend. Isabella and Rudy and their daughters were the other guests. It was late October and the night got chilly, but the party lasted and lasted. The kids all fell asleep in Aleisha's room. The men moved inside to watch a ball game on TV and then a movie on the VCR. Collie Mae brought blankets out onto the porch, and the three women wrapped themselves up and sat and sat, listening to October leaves scuff across the field in the wind and looking up every now and then at the skyful of stars.

Shantee was suddenly overcome by nostalgia and home-sickness. *I can't believe y'all are back here and I'm still out on the high-way. Remember when we were little, and we'd spend the night, and it would be so freezing cold in the morning when we woke up, and we'd all run over by the stove and just hug and hug each other?*

Remember when the fire was all gone out? asked Isabella. *And you'd get up in the morning, and your mother was trying to make a fire, and*

*you'd be trying to get to the washpan 'round the heater and have your sponge
bath and get dressed and go to school?*

Collie Mae was quiet for a long time. *When you say it like that,
it sounds so nice and cozy,* she finally said. *But we don't have to live
like that anymore, and there's lots of people that still do. It has been sicken-
ing to me, since I got home, how many people there are around here that
have even less nowadays than we had back then——a whole lot less. There's
old people, little children, people in shacks, no water, no electricity, no wood
for the heater. I keep thinking it's time to do something.*

The three of them decided right then and there that they
were can-do women who didn't need to just sit around and
talk about things like that. They would form a club. If there
was somebody without heat, this club could bring them a
load of wood or lend them a down payment for a tank of oil.
If somebody's porch steps were broken, or if they had children who needed coats, or if they needed a ride to town to
see if they could get food stamps, or maybe it was just a matter of a sack of groceries to get through the end of the
month——they could help with that. Or if there was somebody that just wanted to learn to write their name and had
never been able to, well, they could help with that, too. They
could help when there was an old person who couldn't get
around anymore without a walker and they couldn't afford a
walker. And in the wintertime, in some of those little old
houses that had no ventilation, the air would get so hot from
the stove you could see the heat waves ripple around the
room, and there would be old people just sitting there like
crabs boiled alive, no fresh air——the club could buy them a
fan, something as simple as that. There were little things that
would make a difference.

Isabella recalled an organization in Newark called Helping Hands, which got them started on a name: *Holding* Hands. That was exactly the idea—holding their neighbors' hands, helping out at a basic level. They would just do what they could do. But, of course, they would do everything the right way: they would need bylaws and dues and fundraising strategies and goals and objectives. They would need another meeting.

They met again two days later, as Shantee and her husband were packing up to head back to the city. The meeting was a hoot: all three women had prepared agendas and proposals written out on yellow legal pads, and all three of them had brought file folders containing model bylaws and sample brochures. From the start, Holding Hands got off on a decidedly businesslike foot.

Dues were set at ten dollars a month, and the initial membership goal was one hundred women per county in three counties. Because Shantee wouldn't be around to help with the work, she contributed five hundred dollars for start-up capital. She also told Isabella and Collie Mae to get in touch with Eula Grant over in Powell County, the daughter of Shantee's mother's old friend Pearl. Eula had been trying to fix up the old community center building in New Jericho, which might work out as a meeting place for Holding Hands or as a location for special events.

By the end of 1981 Holding Hands was incorporated as a tax-exempt nonprofit organization. On Martin Luther King's birthday in January 1982, the club held a memorial ceremony at the newly refurbished community center in New Jericho, which was rededicated that afternoon. A plaque was mounted near the front door, inscribed with the name of Eula Grant, "who gave this community center a new life." The keynote speaker was the president of the state college that Collie Mae had attended. Freshly printed brochures and membership application forms were spread out on a table, and people in the audience signed up on the spot.

In addition to Shantee's start-up money, Holding Hands raised $1,950 in its first year, much of it from a series of raffles; club members who sold twenty-five dollars' worth of raffle tickets in a given month were excused from paying dues for that month. By the end of 1982 they'd reached their goal of one hundred members in Chestnut County and had signed up fifty-eight members in Powell County and thirty-one in Harden County. Because cutting wood had become a major club activity, the bylaws were amended to admit men as members.

The maximum grant for a family was set at two loads of wood plus one hundred dollars, which usually worked out to fifty dollars in cash and fifty dollars in food. Holding Hands also supplied sheets and pillow cases, a high chair, toys, a kitchen table and chairs, whatever people needed. Families whose houses burned up got one hundred dollars plus household items and food.

Once, when Isabella approached a woman who lived on her road about buying a one-dollar raffle ticket, she was told there wasn't a dollar in the house. The woman was taking care of her grandson, and her husband had just died, and she had no money; it also turned out that she had no wood. So Isabella gave her the money she'd collected so far that day from raffle sales, which turned out to be only one dollar, and she arranged to have a load of wood delivered. The next week the woman stopped by Isabella's house and gave her the dollar back.

At the end of the second year Collie Mae wrote up a grant application for Holding Hands and applied for funding from the Z. Smith Reynolds Foundation.

A couple of weeks before we got our first grant, I got three phone calls in one day from people who would not identify themselves. They threatened that we better watch out, we're asking for trouble. Instead of hanging up on them, I asked, "Now, who is this 'we' you're talking about?" And they said, "You just keep your hands to yourself—keep your hands to yourself." In other words, the "we" was Holding Hands. Isabella got calls, too, and she also got letters, and there were at least three letters we know about that were sent to Social Services to try and discredit us. People found notes on their cars. White folks don't want us organizing, but then they never stop talking how we can't do for ourselves. But I say, let's just keep going, 'cause we're helping.

Isabella, meanwhile, was taking her Amway products to every town, every hamlet, every crossroads for miles around. Anywhere she knew anybody—which was virtually everywhere in Chestnut County's six hundred square miles—she sold her wares and visited with the folks and learned about what was going on. One thing she learned was why she was having such a hard time finding a job—why she had been rejected for one job in particular that had sounded like it would be exactly up her alley. The county social services department had advertised for someone with expertise in administering federal funds. Isabella had gotten an interview, but the director had brushed her off immediately, saying that her background was not at all what they needed. She'd been baffled by his rejection until she'd traveled the backroads of the county for a while and realized that Chestnut had no projects whatsoever funded by the federal programs she had been working with in New Jersey. No Head Start, and no day care—zero federal dollars. The only federal money that the county social services office administered went for food stamps and AFDC, even though many other programs existed that were designed specifically for areas with high levels of poverty—a description that fit Chestnut if it fit anywhere. Isabella hadn't yet heard all the explanations of local officials, but she had seen enough to realize that they preferred not to provide the poor people of the county with such services as day care, even if the services could be provided without spending a penny of local money.

About twenty thousand people lived in Chestnut County, 60 percent of them black. Almost 40 percent of the population—nearly eight thousand people—lived below the poverty line. Unemployment was high, but there were many more people working than not working, which to Isabella's way of thinking meant that demand for day-care services must be strong. And most of the jobs in Chestnut and surrounding counties paid minimum wage or thereabouts and offered nothing or next to nothing in the way of employee benefits—which to Isabella's way of thinking meant that unsubsidized day-care services must be way beyond what most working people in Chestnut could afford.

While working her Amway territory, she made a point of visiting all the day-care centers she could find; there were a few around, scattered here and there in private homes, run-down storefronts, and church basements. Conditions in most of the centers shocked her: at one overcrowded proprietary operation called The Three Bears, she noticed missing stair-boards, a broken window with jagged glass at the children's eye level, a jug of bleach sitting out on the bathroom floor, filthy rags used and reused for diaper changing, and Kool-Aid instead of milk at mealtime. Such a place could never pass even a fire inspection, much less meet minimal safety and san-itary standards for a facility jam-packed with young chil-dren—and it had a waiting list. There was no way on earth to improve a center like The Three Bears without spending a great deal of money, and the parents who had no choice but to leave their children there had no way on earth to pay any more.

Isabella knew, however, that the federal government had money available precisely for quality day care in communities too poor to afford it. She knew the money was there, she knew the procedure for applying for it, she knew the criteria for obtaining funding. And even before Collie Mae pointed it out to her, she knew that she as an individual was in a posi-tion to make a big difference in the lives of her friends and neighbors.

She began by documenting the situation. Two food-processing plants in Chestnut County employed more than 1,100 workers, and three other such plants in nearby coun-ties employed 2,000 more. A factory sewing men's underwear employed 210 people, and a furniture maker employed more than 400. Wages in all these industries averaged just over five dollars an hour.

Isabella talked to parents, and she spoke with public offi-cials, who admitted to her face what she had begun to sus-pect: *They said that they turned back these funds year after year. One lady*

told me she didn't believe in government subsidies at all, but her office man-
ages AFDC and food stamps because they have to. In another office the
director said it was a point of pride for him that in his county they served
very few of the eligible families, much fewer than a lot of places. He said
that poor people have more dignity and self-regard for it.

Isabella believed she could organize an effort to bring Title
XX day-care funds to Chestnut County. She knew the people to call upon, and she began to see herself working for
herself and with others—autonomously, drawing on what
she interpreted as the Amway approach.

I bring this attitude to all my work, trying to create an Amway world,
where people believe they can do anything they want to. I could talk about
this all day and all night. When I decided this is what I wanted, I knew it
would happen. I never got uptight about it.

She was not a loner. She called on Collie Mae, of course;
on Eula Grant, who had become a vice president of Holding
Hands; on Menola Rountree with her teen beauty walk organization; and on somebody else recommended by Shantee, a
woman named Maude Allen, who worked as director of
CATS, Chestnut Action for Teenage Students. Shantee said
that Maude was prickly and stand-offish but professional
through and through. They didn't have to like her, but she
was somebody who could make things happen.

At the first meeting Isabella warned everybody that government bureaucracy moved slowly. They gave their organization a name—MAC, Mothers and Children, Inc.—and
they set up a timetable to prepare for the mandated preliminary inspection, with Collie Mae in charge of site selection.
When Maude Allen asked how they planned to obtain the
necessary application forms, Isabella smiled; such a question

demonstrated considerable sophistication about the hard realities of local politics. She'd been thinking about that particular matter a great deal and had concluded that the only way was to circumvent the local social service agencies altogether. MAC, Inc., would have to drive all the way up to the state capital and request the packet of forms in person. *It reminds you of the old days, doesn't it? Remember how our parents used to go over to the food store, the phone company, pay all the bills in person?*

Collie Mae arranged for MAC to use the old Shell gas station in Chowan Springs for their initial demonstration project. They wouldn't have to pay rent, but every inch of the building needed repair and renovation.

The fundraising that followed was like pulling money out of the bottom of the piggy bank. All of the MAC women had overcommitted calendars and overextended bankbooks; they were swamped with work and family and civic obligations. The communities in which they had to raise the money they needed had no money to spare. But none of these problems was new to them. Around Christmastime Collie Mae organized a gift-wrapping booth inside Billie's House of Beauty on Main Street, and Maude Allen and CATS, the youth council, threw a teen dance in Rosedale with a talent show competition. Isabella in Chestnut County and Eula in Powell each set up doughnut sales, bake sales, turkey raffles, fish fries, garage sales. And then there were all the events-after-the-events, the parties and teas and receptions to show appreciation for all the volunteers. The women from Working Women's Curb Market, a produce stand on the highway outside of Chowan Springs, provided MAC with "office" space—a card table and rusty filing cabinet in the storage shed behind the stand—and the men from Dream Land, Collie Mae's cousin's Drive Inn Bar-B-Que, brought ribs to every party.

Working across county lines, MAC focused all its efforts on getting one single model day-care center established. They wrote a grant application and then, eager to lay groundwork for a close working relationship with state officials, they took a preliminary draft in person to the chief deputy director in the Day Care Section of the Department of Human Services in the state capital. After he reviewed their work, they made the suggested changes, and they made a point of calling him about every detail, consulting him on the dotting of every *i* and the crossing of every *t*. Eighteen months later they received official notification of their first grant award.

And that was when the trouble began. Notice of the grant was also sent to the county director of social services in Chowan Springs, a Mrs. Beard, who immediately announced that every penny of that money would be returned to the state. Isabella went over Mrs. Beard's head to her new friend in the state capital.

I worried the chief deputy director to death trying to find out what happened to our funds. We had renovated the building and completely furnished it. There were all the little tables and chairs, and the mats, the toys, the playground. We had interviewed day-care teachers and assistants, and we had begun training. We had checked eligibility and assembled a group of children—not all black children either, it was strictly on income. We had everything but the funds.

The chief deputy director again sent the funds to Chestnut County. This time the social services department passed the buck to the county commissioners, who were supposed to

approve all funds coming into the county. At the Board of
Commissioners meeting, Mrs. Beard made no secret of her
department's opposition to public support of day care. Most
of the commissioners were like-minded, but Maude Allen
had anticipated the precise tone of the meeting and had
made a suggestion that seemed to break the logjam: MAC,
Inc., packed the meeting room with all the little children who
were set to attend the new center. The children sat together
in the first three rows of grown-up-sized chairs, squirming,
occasionally whimpering, and the parents and ministers and
MAC board members who had come prepared to speak never
had to say a word: officially, day-care funding was approved by
a murmured voice vote, and from then on local opposition to
MAC was limited to behind-the-scenes tactics. Bureaucrats
stalled, politicians filed to reduce the allocation, clerks said
they couldn't locate the funds, officials forgot about appoint-
ments and forgot to file papers and forgot how to write a
check. Eventually the commissioners informed MAC that the
funding was secure but that it would be administered by none
other than the county director of social services, their good
friend Mrs. Beard. The MAC women learned to work
through her by sneaking around her and by becoming accustomed to delays, broken promises, unmet deadlines, and the
unmet needs of parents who trusted them.

After three years MAC, Inc., was able to pull the political
levers that changed the procedure for funding so that money
could be allocated directly to their projects. But local attempts
at sabotage continued, and the endless attention they consumed ate at the hearts of the MAC women and nibbled at
the nerves of civic engagement.

When I was coming up, I gave things my best shot. But better than any teacher, even better than my Amway lessons, time is the best teacher, time makes the difference!

Our saving grace was that we created alliances across at least three counties. When this all got started, we could have been in, you know, competition. But then we started helping one another out. If one group was having trouble getting the money—political problems—well, one of us from another county would call the state capital for them, help them out with our direct contacts. We began to train board members in how they could help. We approached our state representative. Only the strong survive.

Shantee Owens missed a MAC board meeting. Her colleagues noted her absence in the manner that the absence of stalwart members from meetings of close-knit organizations is so often noted—by making her the subject of general gossip. By then she'd been back home for three years and was about to become unemployed for a third time—the septic tank company receptionist she'd been replacing was ready to return from maternity leave. It was observed that in recent months she had seemed distracted, a bit short-tempered, and even more aloof than usual. For possible insight, the board members turned to Eula Grant, whose family went way back with Shantee's family.

I don't know of anything right this second, Eula told them. *In fact, from what I hear, her parents are doing a whole lot better lately.*

Better than what?

Oh, now I'm talking out of school, Eula said. *Miss Pearl and Miss Orlonia are going to rip my tongue out.* And that was all she would say.

A visiting anthropologist who happened to be sitting in on

the board meeting took Shantee out to lunch a few days later at the Hardee's on I–95, more than an hour's drive from town. The anthropologist asked a lot of questions, and Shantee told a story.

I never could understand the relationship between my mother and father, because I couldn't understand him. After I moved away, I would ask my mother over and over: Why do you stay with him? Why don't you come to New York and live with me? My mother and I always had a special connection, and when anything went down, she would always call me. I'm always there for her, and for my brothers and sister, too. I'm in the center with all the fury and frenzy.

My mother was always calling me in the middle of the night, so one day my husband and I just took off from work, drove home, and we said to her, "Listen, now you have a decision to make. You can't keep calling in the middle of the night anymore. Just pack your things." We put a U-Haul on the car and brought her up north, and she said she couldn't believe she had left him but she had. She said she'd left him for good.

My husband had tried to talk to my father. When I was younger, I just couldn't talk to him at all, couldn't say anything, but my husband always could. He's a very commonsense kind of person. He just said it straight out—that he wasn't all right with this kind of thing. We don't believe in violence. But you know.

My mother stayed with me for a while. She went to Baltimore with my sister, she stayed with my brother—and then she went back home. They tried it again, and it was the same. I went back home to get her again.

Knowing my mother, you would think that if she's going to have some kind of problem it would not be a communication problem, but in fact that's exactly what it was—there was a total breakdown of communications between the two of them. He said she was supposed to mind him. Which left her in the position, if she was going to be her own person, of not telling him what she was doing, not telling him anything. And then, of course, he would feel like he had nothing to say, so there was no opening there.

Regardless of everything, I don't believe in violence—and he was violent. Nowadays I can say anything to him, and I tell him: "My mother is a grown woman!" He says that his mother had minded his father, that's the way it worked. And I just say it again: "But she's a grown woman."

I'm just not going to say he's all wrong and she's all right. I know it takes two people to make a marriage, and two people to break it up. But he was more wrong than she was, I will say that, because he was violent. And since I've started to stand up to him, I've really thrown him for a loop. I'll talk about anything—like love. I'll say, "How can we know that you love us?" And he'll say, "You should know that because I took care of you." And I'll say, "Well, yeah, you're supposed to do that. There's such a thing as saying 'I love you.' And such a thing as touching and feeling. That's the way I would be with a child of my own."

But these are things he didn't have to draw on from his own childhood, because he was one of the youngest of fifteen children, and the older ones pretty much raised the younger ones, kind of in a real tough manner. Their parents died, and they had to raise each other. By the time I moved back here, I had talked to him a lot, and I understood more about him than I did before I left. I could accept some of his behavior because I knew where it came from.

And I tell my mother all the time: "I am so glad I don't have the dying kind of love that you have." It is unhealthy, you don't need it. I could walk away and never look back, because I know I have something to walk away with. My mother talks a good game, but she never really became self-sufficient—she's too stifled to walk. She was fifteen and he was seventeen when they married, and he thought he was so smooth. He could take on the city. But he was up there for fifteen years and never accomplished anything really, and he came back a very sad man.

*I can walk if I have to because I am independent. And I'm indepen-
dent because I don't have children. I miss that in life. But it's complicated.
My parents are back together again now, and it looked like my father was
shaping up for a while, but it's back to the same old thing. I am so afraid
for my mother sometimes.*

By 1986 MAC was operating three day-care centers in
Chestnut County, one in Powell County, and two in nearby
Harden County. Rose Towers, Sunshine Center, Toddlers Club
House, Lady Bug, Children's Wonderland, Rainbow Early
Learning, and Teddy Bear Town were all safe and sanitary
child-care facilities, with trained staffs, developmentally ori-
ented curricula, parent participation on the boards, and slid-
ing fee schedules. More than three hundred children were
enrolled. Fifty new full-time jobs and a couple of dozen
part-time jobs were created directly to staff the centers, and
the availability of the centers enabled many parents to hold
jobs for the first time, bringing thousands of additional dollars into the community.

Isabella became MAC's paid director. Shantee Owens was
hired to manage Lady Bug Day Care Center.

7

Mother's Day

MAC, Inc., and Holding Hands bleed the poor to help the poor. But they also represent a new type of organizing activity in poor rural communities. Serious and sustainable services in desperately poor rural counties cannot succeed on turkey raffles and fish fries alone. They cannot be funded solely or even largely by charitable contributions from the tiny handful of black business and professional people in these communities. They might be aided to a degree by local tax support, but political resistance is unyielding. They might be aided significantly by large industries employing local people, but the history is bleak: corporate operations in places like Powell and Chestnut counties have never supported local organizations in the black community.

People who return and get involved feel they have to go it alone. One morning a four-year-old boy at Teddy Bear Town waved at a car that was driving by, and one of his classmates ran inside the center and hid. *You can't wave to a white person,* the terrified child told his teacher. *They'll shoot off your hands. They'll kill you.* Some adults remain almost that fearful; it may take more than a wave, they argue, but there is a degree of speaking out that will put a black person's life at risk. Other people believe that fear is more a white man's tool than a danger to black lives. The women of Holding Hands felt the threats against them reflected white efforts to intimidate them, which is not quite the same as actual efforts to maim or kill them.

Obviously, the new old South isn't the old old South, but distrust, fear, and hostility persist. In the midst of so much bitterness and ill will, outside money is a critical resource. Dogged self-help, with no reliance on government funding, can support some small initiatives, such as Holding Hands— although even Holding Hands eventually needed outside money, for which they turned to charitable foundations. Even a hundred such organizations, however, can't do it all.

Where large numbers of people lack the minimal necessities of life, public funds make a difference. Organizing by black women (and men) to help provide obviously needed services— firewood, say, or safe child care—is perceived by "the white community" as threatening rather than helpful. An outsider might suggest that within the white community are surely as many nuances and varieties of opinion as exist within the black community, but it often doesn't sound that way to a black person listening to the discussion at county commission meetings.

Collie Mae and Isabella and the other activists feel that the white establishment routinely, almost reflexively, tries to tear down whatever they build up, and that the strategies of white resistance are as old as Jim Crow. They say their biggest headache, year in and year out, has been the resistance of white bureaucrats who could have been allies. When bureaucratic habits of inaction and insensitivity are compounded by old racist habits of resistance and recoil, headaches can last a long time.

Collie Mae and Isabella are organizers. People who never left Chestnut County have also formed organizations around social issues but never to the same extent, or the same effect. The people returning home brought experience with structures and strategies that established them locally as people to be contended with. They created networks and coalitions that grew.

In the scholarly literature, this sort of work has been termed social-capital formation, a notion that has recently attracted public attention as a key to community uplift. The new public interest is ironic on four or five levels: for one thing, it comes along at a moment when observers have widely acknowledged a drastic decline, throughout the United States, in participation in neighborly or other voluntary associations. As at the turn of this century, perhaps, when scholars suddenly began to discuss the significance of the frontier in American life, interest seems to dawn as an era comes to a close. Uprootedness, which is related to migration, of course, among other modern habits, may contribute to—or result from—the loss of social ties. Nonetheless, a second level of irony involves the political response to the decline of voluntarism: a reduction in the public assistance that might supplement or substitute for weakened private service organizations.

A third irony is that the generation returning to rural homeplaces today—the repeatedly uprooted, the people who might be termed least suited for developing social relationships grounded in neighborliness—are the very people forging serious civic and associational involvements in these communities.

Yet a fourth irony is that, at least in places like Chestnut County, the people who proclaim most loudly the urgency and legitimacy of self-help, the bureaucrats and politicians, are the same people who, when faced with actual self-help organizations in their home communities, work to thwart them.

A fifth irony—or perhaps *irony* as a label is too elegant and neat—a last question, perhaps, or dilemma, spins on migration itself. People come into the modern world from all sorts of places; if they then choose to leave modern metropolitan life to go back home again, should they be considered uprooted, displaced, refugees—the victims, in a sense, of modernism? Or is it those among us who no longer have homeplaces and kin to return to who represent the shocking emblems of the end of modernity?

Everyone considers Maude Allen a modern woman. She doesn't hide her light under a bushel basket, she doesn't close her eyes or her ears to avoid facing the truth. And Maude gets things done. She has a B.A. in public administration and provides valuable technical assistance to several organizations in the region; she works tirelessly on behalf of every club and movement and coalition in the county; and she serves on the board of directors of MAC, Inc., and several other groups. How does she do it all? *Not the way you might think,* she explains. Nothing in a little place like Rosedale is ever the way it looks. Nothing ever really happens out in public; it's always, always, always what goes on in the back rooms that matters.

Maude shares her home with her grandfather, her six children, and a widowed brother and his son. Every one of them will sit you down and tell you that Maude is just like her grandmother, who was an active and unforgettable force in the Rosedale sit-ins in the 1960s. She's a woman who's got a mind of her own, they will say, and she's a woman who's going to make a difference someday in Chestnut County. And the way she will do it, everybody will tell you, what really sets Maude Allen apart from your everyday wanna-be, is that Maude Allen is *organized.* She's an organizational genius.

It all started with ironing numbers on football jerseys. One summer when Maude was a teenager, she participated in an Upward Bound group that spent six weeks on a college campus. All the students were expected to help earn their keep by working on campus, and Maude was assigned to the athletic director's office, where she ironed on the numbers, learned to operate a copy machine, and taught herself to type. At the end of the summer, when the group returned to Rosedale and completed an assignment helping the junior high school principal clean the school windows, Maude responded eagerly to a request for volunteer assistance in the school office. After the principal saw how competently she could type and file and fill out forms, he gave her one of the biggest thrills of her young life: she was asked to assist him in working out class schedules. She assigned homeroom teachers, filled out the class rosters and the individual schedule cards, registered pupils for required courses and optional electives—and felt a sudden rush of power. After school opened she went back to the office every day during her study hall to prepare absentee lists and lunchroom tickets, track teachers' timesheets, and process paperwork for students transferring in or out of the school.

One office skill just led to another. When I went to college, I worked in the Athletic Department, and the director made me the sports information director. People would write the school for information, and I would put the statistics together and mail off the data to pro scouts or whoever requested it. When the college ran a summer youth sports program, I helped organize it—I took care of all the logistics, the scheduling, dorm assignments, transportation, meals, everything. We had children coming in from five different counties, and that was when I really learned what's involved in making things run smoothly. I learned a lot.

After college Maude moved to Washington, D.C., and was hired to run playtime activities for a large day-care program. She expected to love the job, but she hated it: the little children didn't let her organize them the way the older kids had in the youth sports program. Toddlers wouldn't listen, and even when they listened, they wouldn't just shut their mouths and get with the program. When she said, *Sit*, they'd say, *How come?*

Another problem with that job was that the playground

the children were supposed to use was part of a recreation center run by a man named Warner T. Allen, Jr., who wouldn't leave her alone. In later years she decided that what happened was that she'd married him mainly to stop him from harassing her so much about marrying him. In the meantime, however, she went hunting for another job.

She decided she'd rather work with older children, and so she applied to all the public school systems in the Washington area. The D.C. system hired her, but somehow she wound up in the central office instead of a classroom; for twelve years she sat at a desk processing expense vouchers. Every day of those twelve years she sat at her desk and shuffled papers and daydreamed about better jobs.

At first she imagined herself as the manager of something, maybe a big department store, planning what to buy and how much to sell it for and how to display it, how to advertise. But then she got married and started having babies and her life began to seem, well, stressful. Even an organizational genius can be challenged by six babies in nine years, plus a full-time job, plus a husband who never ran out of things to harass her about. And with so much stress and commotion in her life, even daydreaming at her desk seemed to consume so much energy that Maude felt she had to ration it; she could allow herself little dreams now, but not big ones, and they had to stick close to home. Even her idle imagination, she figured, shouldn't be wasted. She might as well take charge of her daydreams, turn them in a more practical direction—and who knows?

So she imagined herself organizing a youth athletic league, hundreds and hundreds of girls and boys, all with uniforms and sports equipment and strong, graceful bodies, and with innocent and hopeful little hearts imbibing important lessons in teamwork and self-discipline. As her own children grew older and her thoughts settled more and more on the hard lessons awaiting them, her daydreaming became even more of an extension of what she was fretting about as a mother. In her dream job she would follow children out from home into the world, taking over where parents left off to lead them toward useful, fulfilling lives in the community. For a few important weeks of Maude's own teenage life, Upward Bound had functioned in exactly that way for her, and now she ached to see more leadership, more guidance, more adult investment in young people.

But all she did every day was go to work and stop by the store on the way home and feed her kids and wash their clothes and try to check their homework and keep after them and try to deal with Warner. If he hadn't walked out on her on the first birthday of their sixth child—he just went home to his mother, perhaps because (as she theorized in later years) after ten years he seemed to have finally run out of ideas for things to harass her about—if she hadn't been left alone to raise six children in a bad neighborhood in what still felt like a strange city, hundreds of miles from home, she'd probably have gone on indefinitely sitting at her desk every day and daydreaming.

But something had to change, so Maude sent her baby and her next-to-youngest back home to her grandmother, and with help from one of her sisters who lived in Maryland just outside Washington, she and the four oldest children hung on in D.C. for two more years. But that was all she could take.

When she returned home, at the age of thirty-five, she still looked young and slender, not like anybody's stereotype of a harassed mother of six. And she was determined to start living her own life her own way, even if it meant she had to start from square one and invent her own kind of wheel.

She started going to meetings. She dressed as if she were still going to work in a city office, wearing shoes that matched her suits and lipstick that matched her nail polish. No one at the Board of Education meetings in the East Chestnut High School gym looked half so stylish; nor, for that matter, did anyone at the county Board of Commissioners meetings in the courthouse. After sitting in on every public meeting in Chestnut County for more than a year, watching and learning and certainly being seen, Maude Allen started making the rounds to introduce herself.

And then she made her presentation. At a Board of Commissioners meeting, Maude requested appointment of a task force on expanding services to youth. The role of the task force would be to seek private and public funding and charter a youth council.

After her speech she presented the commissioners with a printed and bound copy of her twenty-page proposal, accompanied by letters of recommendation from all of the right people in the county. The superintendent of schools and two school principals wrote letters of support; the sheriff signed a notice endorsing her plan; an editorial in the local newspaper supported the scheme as an approach to preventing delinquency; and parents testified on behalf of the proposal as an attempt to keep their children in school. Maude requested that the Board of Commissioners pay her a half-time salary, six thousand dollars, to chair the task force while she worked to raise outside funds.

Now I run my own show. I'm my own boss. We have created a youth council in Chestnut County that the teenagers named CATS, which stands for Chestnut Action for Teenage Students. Young people are going to have a voice in this county, especially when decisions are made that relate to them. You know, they have voices, but nobody ever thought about hearing them. In CATS they are being trained to think politically. That's certainly something my generation was never taught. These kids are asking questions! Unfortunately, their teachers are not good role models, because they don't become involved. They're scared for their jobs, scared of the system, and they pass that fear on to their students.

Within a year, Maude Allen received outside funding for CATS, three small grants from statewide corporate foundations totaling about twelve thousand dollars. The county also increased its support, to ten thousand dollars. CATS set up a youth hotline so that teenagers could provide phone counseling and referrals for other teenagers. A part-time counselor was hired as a liaison between the county sheriff's office and the families of youth offenders. What Maude never emphasized, however, in her appeals for financial support were certain other CATS activities that edged the teenagers over into—in fact, tumbled them head over heels into the center of—the arena of political action.

Jerome Harris from Rosedale is running for county commissioner this year. I think there are a lot of people in the county who are going to be supportive, because they are tired of not being represented. That makes voter registration very important.

So this morning I asked the school principal over at East Chestnut High School if I could do a voter registration project at school—you know, some-

thing educational, about the importance of registering, and how to register. And he said okay. Now, from his point of view, it will be educational, and that's correct, the students will be learning. But they'll also be registering to vote, right there in the school gym, all the ones that are eighteen; I'll be over there until second period signing them up. And then the ones that aren't eighteen yet, they can sign up, too, for the youth teams I am going to be sending out into the county, all over this county, to get people registered to vote. No one's doing anything about getting the vote out, and blacks are nearly 59 percent in Chestnut. You would never guess it from our voting record.

I have become very intrigued by politics here of late. I know that the only way to make big changes is to get in a decision-making position. You have to use the skills that God gave you, and you gotta know when to smile. I've done what I had to do to get what I wanted. I have always been self-sufficient and able to take care of myself. I have always been my own person.

When I was away, I gave a lot of thought to what I wanted to do with my life. And one thing I realized was that when you try to spend your whole life satisfying other people, it doesn't work. It never works. People have to satisfy themselves, you can't do it for them. And if you don't think about satisfying yourself—what you, yourself, want to do—then nobody's going to be able to do it for you. This is something I try to teach my own children, and all the CATS kids. And one of the things I came up with for me, personally, is that I would rather be in the role of leader than follower. I'll be a follower when I have to, but when I can be a leader, that's all the better.

In this county, as far as getting youth involved in anything like politics, that just never happened. Folks here, they sit back even when they have nothing to be scared about. It shouldn't have taken this long to get more than what we have. We need more positive thinking. That's something I try to teach to the young people I work with.

When I moved back, I was extremely disappointed. If I had come back here with the same attitude that I left with in my twenties, I would be just like the people that lived here who had never gone anywhere. But I came back different. I know when they are dumping on us, and I call their attention to it. I talk to them in a diplomatic way, but I say "Hey, this is not the way it's supposed to be." And you know, they back off when they know you'll call them on it.

In D.C., I wouldn't say that I was a leader, but I came back here with certain knowledge, and some skills, and a lot of work experience, life experience. The only problem is that, down here, nothing can be direct. I have found it a major challenge and a pain in the neck. Down here, to get anything done you have to go about it delicately, and a lot of times you have to be very innovative. Even something that should be reasonably easy, it's not going to happen the easy way. People here just don't think like I do. They don't figure on alternate ways of working through problems. They get easily frustrated and overwhelmed. They have never been exposed to success.

In 1986 Maude Allen was among the organizers of a Mother's Day banquet in honor of Mrs. Menola Rountree, who had been active in numerous community organizations for thirty years or more and was about to retire from her position as home economics teacher at East Chestnut High School. I was among the sixty men and women invited to the affair, and so was my mother, who was then seventy-seven years old and visiting with me for Mother's Day weekend. My mother had gotten to know Mrs. Rountree during another visit about a year earlier, when my mother had made her first trip to Chowan Springs. The two women seemed happy to see each other again and quickly settled down to talk in the foyer outside the banquet room.

Because many of the guests were driving forty miles or more to come to the banquet, which was scheduled for the Saturday night before Mother's Day, half or more of the motel rooms were reserved for banquet guests. A big weekend was in the making. Taking advantage of the gathering of out-of-towners, MAC, Inc., had arranged to hold its annual board of directors meeting in the banquet room at 5:00 P.M., about two hours before the evening's main event. As the MAC people congregated before the meeting, the treasurer pulled out the organization's checkbook and began writing checks to board members to reimburse them for expenses they described to her.

Now, wait just a minute here, Maude Allen interrupted. *I don't see any receipts for these so-called expenses. Where are the receipts? Why should we be paying money out of our own treasury without getting a receipt? That's no way to run a business.*

The treasurer and chairperson tried to brush off the criticism. *Oh, now, Maude, you understand how it is, now just sit down and relax. These are just little incidental expenses, no big deal, just reimbursing the people who spent out of pocket. All right? Now, this meeting is called to order, and at the top of the agenda . . .*

Little incidental expenses? What are you talking about? I didn't see any of this nonsense in the 1986 budget we approved. I swear, there've been eight, ten checks written out tonight. Now you add that up—it all adds up. Don't you understand about budgets?

Maude, now calm down. It's just the way we've been doing. Our first item on the agenda . . .

But this is ignorant. If we're not going to follow our own budget, how are we ever going to get anything accomplished?

Maude, I'm sorry, but I'm going to have to say you're out of order just now, because before we can do anything about the budget, we have to elect two more board members for next year. So the first item on the agenda, if y'all will refer to the handout, you'll see the two names in nomination, now all in favor . . .

Menola Rountree and another long-time board member were scheduled to rotate off the board that summer. The people who had been nominated to replace them were like Menola in many ways: older women, from families that had been doing pretty well in the area for many years—families that had received the stamp of approval, so to speak, from the local white establishment. There had always been a handful of black families and individuals whom white politicians and businesspeople had turned to for one reason or another—if they wanted information, say, about someone in the black community or if they were interested in somebody's land-holdings. The families that served this function were rewarded sometimes: Menola Rountree, for example, had gotten a job as home economics teacher after her father had deeded over two acres of his land for a dollar an acre so that the county could build a water tower. When the water lines were laid, however, back in the late 1940s, they skirted the black community near the new tower and served only the white neighborhoods in town.

When MAC, Inc., was first organized, there had been no question about the importance of including board members from the traditional "patron" families. And Menola Rountree defended the practice as she prepared to retire: *You always have to have some of the old-timers on the board. It won't look right, you know, if it seems like MAC is nothing but a bunch of outsiders, newcomers.*

And besides, there's certain ones in town that will talk to us, and they won't talk to just anybody. We can be the eyes and ears. There's a value in it.

Maude Allen hit the ceiling. *That is exactly what's wrong with this whole organization. The olden ways are what's gotten us into this mess today. You say it's just a couple of tokens to please the white folk, but that's not all it is. It's going on and doing everything the old-fashioned way, still keeping everything the same as it was done way back when, never thinking about the future, no planning, no financial safeguards, no nothing. It's just ignorant, that's all. What we need on this board are professionals.*

To every name, every motion, Maude objected—and she had allies around the table; she had seen to that beforehand. Finally, she stood up, walked to the head of the table, and essentially took over the meeting:

MAC, Incorporated, needs people who can do professional work; we are in dire need of long-range financial planning. How can we expect granting agencies to respect our way when we do the way we do? What's going to happen if we get audited? This old-fashioned, simple-minded way we spend money is just the recipe for disaster.

We need a financial plan—for five years, for one year—and we need a monthly budget. We need to have all our accounts set up for the different expenditures, and then when the account runs out, that's it, we just stop writing checks. If there's something unexpected, that's what reserves are for. We don't even have any reserves. If you want to be reimbursed, you need to turn in your receipt. This is the twentieth century. We can't keep fooling around.

I don't see how we can afford to wait any longer; these next slots on the board need to be filled by people who have got the appropriate skills. And for that matter, we need a treasurer who's got some experience with all this sort of thing. And I apologize to present company, but that's just the way it is.

Present company, in the form of the current treasurer, who was no professional accountant and in fact was struggling to keep formal books for the first time in her life, was not inclined to accept the apology. Without a word, she gathered her papers, and checkbook, and left the room. The hurt look on her face turned the tide; the chairperson immediately declared Maude out of order, the original nominees were approved by a comfortable margin, Maude slipped back into her seat without another word, and the treasurer was reelected for another year.

Maude lost the battle. The next year, however, she would try again and win.

In the meantime, the meeting adjourned, and board members headed for their rooms to change clothes and freshen their makeup before the banquet. Maude Allen was among the many speakers that night who spoke glowingly of Menola Rountree's long career of service, of her wisdom and dedication, and the two women embraced tearfully and gave every public indication of utterly disregarding that little ol' quibble back in the board meeting. Mrs. Rountree accepted flowers and certificates and plaques from the crowd, and finally a trophy: a statue of a seated woman with children gathered around her.

After the banquet, while the waiters and buspeople cleared the tables and rearranged the furniture in the hall, Mrs. Rountree and my mother settled into adjacent chairs in the middle of the room and began to talk. The thrust of their conversation was the value of time, and patience, in determining what really mattered in life. They swapped stories of incidents that had once seemed all-important but had later proved trivial. As the dishes and favors and flowers disappeared from around them, their voices went on and on, recounting story after story, always with the same theme: Time will tell. Patience heals.

Maude Allen, along with Isabella and Collie Mae and Shantee and the MAC treasurer and several other board members, began carrying their chairs over near the women talking in the middle of the room. Eventually chairs encircled the storytellers, who were clearly offering commentary, in their indirect way, on the events of the early part of the evening.

No one argued. Everyone seemed to want to believe them. The voices of contention were hushed, for the moment.

8

Election Day

The morning I first met Donald Hardy, in his uncle's diner in Burdy's Bend, he had tried to explain to me how the return of so many of his neighbors and friends was going to change everything. I was inclined at the time to dismiss his remarks—delusions of grandeur, I suspected. I even teased him a little about having stars in his eyes. But a couple of years later I went back for another breakfast at Uncle Slim's, and I asked him to bring me up to date on his views.

Oh, my views haven't changed any, he told me. *Someday you'll come down here to Chestnut County, and you won't recognize the place. Not anytime soon, but eventually. Bottom rail on top—it'll happen.*

You've heard people talk about a second Reconstruction. I guess it was the civil rights movement, when that idea came in. The first Reconstruction didn't take root, and so the thinking is, well, maybe that was partly our own fault, we hadn't laid the groundwork. Maybe it wasn't only a matter of how they had the guns and we didn't.

But I'm not sure I go along with that theory. Because really, what killed off Reconstruction? What did they call those folks? The Redeemers. The white people who felt like they were getting robbed—they were losing control. In Reconstruction, they'd been shoved off to the side, and they rose up and made a power play, right? They said they were "redeeming" their rightful place—taking back their land.

And the way I see it, that's how we need to look at it today—not a second Reconstruction but a second Redemption. We're the ones now that have been shoved aside, we're the folk who've gotten everything robbed from us. And we just have to move in and say: "This is ours, it's rightfully ours. It's our land, too."

Uncle Slim interrupted. *What land you talking about?* he asked. *Do I look like I've died and left you any land?*

Donald told me later that Uncle Slim is trying to retire. During breakfast every morning Slim tries to talk his nephew into taking over the Brooklyn Diner. *You're barking up the wrong tree,* Donald tells him. *I know that,* says Slim. *I guess I know every tree in this neighborhood, and you may be the wrong tree, but you're a good one. You just go out and give 'em hell today.*

Donald says he tries. Every day he tries to give 'em a little hell. As part of his job as Powell County's regional planner, he is an ex officio member of the Eastern Carolina Regional Development Council. Theoretically he provides technical assistance, helping potential industries select sites, meet their needs for water, electricity, or transportation upgrades, develop training programs in cooperation with local schools, negotiate tax-incentive packages, and work out possible conflicts, such as competition with local businesses for customers or employees. But actually, on most days, what Donald really does is sit at the table with the other council members and try to find out what they've been doing behind his back.

His number-one priority, he says, is jobs—more jobs and better jobs. It's a 90–10 situation, the way he looks at it: Ninety percent or more of the black people working in Powell and surrounding counties are earning five dollars an hour or less, and 10 percent or fewer of them get health insurance, pensions, or any other employee benefits. He'd like to see those numbers switched.

The only way to do that is to bring in new industry, new economic blood. Recently Donald spent an entire year negotiating with a manufacturer whose plant could have employed as many as two hundred people in Powell County. He put so much energy into the project and developed such a robust working relationship with the owner of the company that for once he broke his own rule and allowed himself to feel optimistic. By the end of the year all the *i*s were dotted and *t*s were crossed except for a single trivial detail involving the length of the company's lease on acreage in the tax-supported but heretofore-unoccupied county industrial park. Donald had easily worked out the terms and prepared the whole package for formal approval. The cat was in the bag.

But at the meeting he couldn't even get the council members to discuss the proposal, much less vote on it. They kept changing the subject, as if he weren't in the room. *Look,* he finally said, when it became obvious that the whole project was down the drain. *I'm going to need something to tell this man. He's expecting to move here.* There was a brief silence, then some whispering, and nobody would meet his eyes. *Well, Mr. Hardy,* somebody finally said, still not looking him in the eye. *I think you need to say to him whatever you in your professional judgment decide you need to say to him. It's really not the sort of thing this council had ought to get into.*

At that point, Donald tried to give 'em hell. They listened quietly and then went on to other business. As best he could piece things together later, the council members had simply reached the conclusion, perhaps during a golf game the weekend before the meeting, that this particular employer would probably exert upward pressure on wages in Powell County.

Long before there's ever a public meeting, decisions have already been made. If a business is unionized, the Industrial Development Council won't have it. If a business pays more than minimum wage, the council won't have it—they feel like their own operations are at stake, because if one place is paying higher wages, then either that's where all the best employees are going to wind up or else everybody's going to have to pay higher wages. And a lot of the industries around here, poultry and textiles and so on, are so cutthroat that the employers are afraid a higher wage would just sink them.

So there's an element of the white community that is absolutely an unmovable obstacle. They don't want new jobs, they don't want better jobs, and they'll fight to prevent it. And the position they're in, they can win a fight like that. There's no way to work around them or to get something done when they don't want it. I have been sitting at the table with those people now for five years, and I have worked my butt off, and I have tried everything in the book. But if they don't want to hear it, they don't hear it. It really is as simple as that: they call the shots.

*How do we change that? I mean, suppose we could elect our own offi-
cials and maybe even get a majority on the Industrial Development Council and so forth. Would anything be any different? In a way, that's the
wrong question, because the tremendous apathy in our community keeps us
from electing people. In this county there are nine hundred more black voters registered than white voters, but every election they elect an ignorant old
white man over his black opponents—and there have been some very well-
qualified opponents. We don't have the grassroots leadership. The ministers
and the funeral directors—the ones that have always been the power bro-
kers between us and the white folk—why would they want to give that up?
And the rest of the community, they've learned since they were little children that life is just a whole lot simpler if you don't rock the boat. People
won't get involved.*

*But if we did start winning some elections—I mean on a major
scale—I'm still not positive how much it would help. The more progressive
industries, they take one look at a place like New Jericho, and they say,
"Where are the schools? We want educated, well-trained employees. And
where's the infrastructure? Where's the cultural activities for me and my
family?" And then there's always some businesses that won't even take that
first look. There's just too many black folk around here. The story I heard
about one factory that the council was going after, the owner said, and I
quote, "Oh, I don't believe my wife would be comfortable in a place like
that."*

*I guess if black people owned the factories, we wouldn't be up against
that particular situation. But we don't own much of anything. Look at my
uncle's café. It's not all that much of anything, but it's for sale, and there's
nobody in the county with the money to buy it. And do you really think
there's a bank around here that would make a loan on it? We don't have the
capital, the expertise, and we don't have the banks to support us. And so it*

doesn't matter what we want or what we do, we aren't going to be involved in the decision making.

I'm not saying there hasn't been any progress at all, but we haven't even taken the first steps toward getting control of our own development. Our economic development is all in the hands of white people—and I mean totally in their hands.

Next door to Rosedale Elementary is a red-brick building that was built at the turn of the century to serve as Chestnut County's teachery, a dorm-style residence that provided room, board, and chaperones for single young women who had left their home communities to teach school. The teachery has now been remodeled and rented out to the state Employment Security Commission, which uses it as a branch office open three mornings a week, with other hours by appointment. The Rosedale branch, which since the late 1960s has been staffed by the same individual, Mrs. Samantha Jones, provides information on job opportunities in the area but does not process applications for unemployment compensation. People wishing to file for those benefits are referred to the main county office in Chowan Springs.

Mrs. Jones says the character of Chestnut County's economy has changed dramatically since she got into this line of work. In the 1960s unemployment was low, and 70 percent of local residents were employed in agriculture; today unemployment is high, and 70 percent of the jobs are industrial. Employers in the county pay between minimum wage and $5.50 an hour. Even though the work employers offer is often temporary or seasonal in nature, they are looking for employees with a steady work history; according to Mrs. Jones, workers who have gone from job to job in the hopes of getting ahead generally do not appeal to local employers.

The people returning from up north often do better in the job market than people who stayed at home, Mrs. Jones believes. They are better educated, and they have more extensive work histories and a clearer sense of what kind of work they want. They have to take pay cuts, but in Mrs. Jones's experience, they all understand that already and don't need her to explain it to them. She estimates that people typically find the wages back home about 20 or 25 percent less than the wages they are accustomed to, though they can hope eventually for raises and promotions that will help them recover some of the loss.

As a rule, Mrs. Jones has noted, high school students don't want to go north.

The girls, especially, want to stay, but a few of the boys still go off, not so much up north, but maybe to Columbia or Greensboro. They feel like that's the only chance they've got for finding work, but from what I've seen, it seems like it doesn't usually go all that well for them. For one thing, our southern cities have just as much drugs and gangs and so on. A lot of the young people that do leave end up coming home again anyway.

And the younger generation staying around here, their being here gives this office an even bigger challenge. The job opportunities here for young people are just not that appealing. And a lot of our youth have deficiencies when it comes to applying for work.

A lot of the young people just don't know very much about opportunities here locally, so one thing we try to do is have a jobs fair that goes around to the high schools. We're not going to do the fair here at East Chestnut— it's an incredible amount of work, and my manager had to make the decision—but we did have it here one time, maybe seven or eight years ago. And we have a three-week program we run that is called Job Club, where we teach our disadvantaged youth about the skills they need to find a job— the grooming, appearance, filling out applications, interviewing.

Right now, I'll tell you, the unemployment rate for women is 14 percent, and that's what it's been running, 13.7, 14.7. This is black women I'm talking about. For men, it runs 8.8. The problem for women is that they can't do heavy work. Women have got better education than the men, in your typical case, but all the work for women is sewing, a little bit of wood products, and right now three shifts of poultry. For the women coming back from up north, if they've got good communication skills, then maybe clerical work—otherwise poultry.

Chestnut County has been depressed economically for the past ten or fifteen years—and really, to tell you the truth, we've been poor here forever. But it's just getting sadder and sadder in this county. It seems like in the last few years this place has just died.

We are very far behind when it comes to attracting good jobs. Education is a problem. Our educated people do not come back; it's the poor people who come back, or else rich people coming to retire. We don't have the skilled jobs, professional jobs, for educated people. And the reason we don't have those jobs . . . I'll tell you what it is: employers won't come here. They say the workforce has deficiencies. And I'll tell you what they mean by deficiencies, because I've heard white people say it. It means we're a majority-black people around here.

What we do have is a plentiful and trainable workforce with low salary expectations.

Vernon Bradley and his wife Emily both have a history of stable, long-term employment. After earning their teaching certificates at the State University of New York at Buffalo, they came home for two years; Vernon taught history at the old Booker T. Washington High School near Rosedale, and Emily taught English. They then returned to Vernon's high school alma mater up in Harlem, where for the next twenty years they both served on the faculty. After accumulating twenty years' worth of contributions to their retirement plans, Vernon and Emily, who were then in their mid-forties, were able to obtain a fairly substantial loan from their teachers' credit union, putting up their pensions as collateral. They quit their jobs and moved back to Chowan Springs, where they built a house with part of the money and made arrangements to invest the rest in a business partnership proposed by Vernon's younger sister Veronica.

Veronica was much younger than Vernon—not even thirty yet. She had a fourteen-year-old son, but he represented an earlier stage of her life, a period she'd been trying to put behind her. With Vernon's help, she had obtained a college degree in public administration and then supported herself and her son for several years working as a secretary in the dean's office of the college she'd attended. Since returning home, about two years before Vernon, she had not been able to find a good job, but she had come up with an intriguing business idea: she and Vernon and Emily could open up a copy shop in Chowan Springs. The churches would be obvious customers, the black churches anyway. Vernon and Emily had the capital, and Veronica had the time.

Only it turned out that Vernon and Emily really didn't have the capital. Their house cost more to build than they'd planned, and day-to-day living expenses kept exceeding what they'd expected. True, most things cost less in Chowan Springs than in New York, but not enough less. Emily had gotten a temporary job typing names for the phone book, but a couple of trips to the dentist had swallowed up that income. Veronica got a little irritated when they tried to explain all this.

Vernon really did want to help her out. He also wanted to help his nephew, Veronica's son Kendrick, who was starting high school at East Chestnut. He volunteered to accompany Kendrick to freshman registration, figuring that, as a former high school teacher himself, he would be in a good position to see that Kendrick signed up for the right courses and got hooked up with the best teachers.

But there was really nothing for him to do. East Chestnut offered so few courses that Kendrick basically had no choices to worry about, and to the extent that Vernon could identify the best of the teachers, he was not impressed with any of them. Within a few minutes of the start of registration, two boys were summarily suspended from school for three days for wearing T-shirts with sports-team logos. When they argued that they'd thought the dress code applied only to regular school days, the principal said they were being insolent and added an extra day to their suspension.

Vernon also noticed numerous children turned away from the registration tables because they owed fees from the previous year: $6.74 for a damaged math book, $2.25 bus fare for a required field trip, a $5.00 locker rental fee. Fees were also being assessed for the coming year, and some children were turned away because the money they'd brought with them wasn't enough. One girl broke into tears when she was told she'd need $45.50 for science class supplies, PE clothes, and a damage deposit for use of the computer lab.

Another girl was accompanied at the registration table by a woman who looked so young Vernon thought at first she must be another high school pupil. But she was the girl's aunt, and she was furious at school officials: *What is this nonsense about tuition? It's a public school. It's a Chestnut County school, and my niece lives right here in Chestnut County with me. She doesn't have to pay no $200 tuition.* The person behind the table said tuition fees were required to enroll students whose parents lived outside the county; the girl's mother lived in Philadelphia. *Well, I don't have your $200,* the aunt said. *So I guess my niece just won't be going to your school.* The registrar asked her to wait a moment while she went over to another table for a brief whispered conversation. When she returned, she told the aunt that her niece could be enrolled on a provisional basis; the school would send the tuition bill to the parents up north. The registrar dropped the girl's registration forms into a box on her table labeled "tuition drawer."

On his way out of the school gym, Vernon stopped by the desk where a white parent was signing up PTA members. He paid for three memberships: one in Veronica's name and two for Emily and himself. While he was filling out the paperwork, another white parent came over and struck up a conversation with the first PTA parent about the county's new private school, Chestnut Christian Academy. The two of them were updating each other as to which of their friends' children were going to CCA and which ones were still in public school. Vernon picked up his papers and moved a few feet away so he could eavesdrop.

It was discouraging. Every year the number of white students at East Chestnut kept dropping. Chestnut Christian, it seemed, offered more of everything, better everything, and there were no discipline problems. Kids who didn't shape up, didn't apply themselves, were just kicked out. Vernon looked around at the handful of white students in the gym and wondered how many of them were rejects from Chestnut Christian. He also wondered if he oughtn't try to send Kendrick there.

Bracing himself, he asked the PTA parents how much the private school cost. But they didn't respond at all the way he expected. In fact, they were not just cordial, they almost gushed over him when he confided his concern that East Chestnut might not offer Kendrick the quality of education Vernon wanted for him. *Oh, if only the other parents were like you,* they told him. The academy cost two thousand dollars a year, not counting books, but he shouldn't worry, there were still ways for children to get an excellent education in the public schools. There were problems nowadays, that was to be expected, but in the honors classes . . .

The honors classes? What honors classes? Vernon strode back over to the registration area and requested a conference with the principal.

Two years later, in 1980, Vernon Bradley was elected as the first black member of the Chestnut County School Board. In his campaign he promised fairness in school discipline, more access to advanced courses at the high schools, an end to tuition and student fees, more black teachers and administrators, and cleaner, better-maintained school buildings.

Kendrick, meanwhile, had been doing well in his honors courses, though he complained that all the faculty members assigned to teach those classes were white. But he wasn't doing so well with his basketball, which he said was his life. When he didn't make the team, he complained about the white coach. Even though Vernon complained that Kendrick complained too much, Vernon also called the basketball coach at Chestnut Christian to see if anything could be arranged. Apparently nothing could.

The county public schools were then 80 percent black; Chestnut Academy was about 98 percent white, enrolling just two black students. Some white parents believed that even the academy wasn't good enough for their children, and there were carpools in Chowan Springs that carried some white children to private schools in distant counties.

Nothing infuriated Vernon more as a school board member than to have to listen to those carpooling parents speak at school board meetings. They claimed to be taxpayers, some of them even claimed to be interested in improving the schools, and Vernon had no trouble understanding how a decent, caring parent might want to consider private education. But it seemed obvious to him that once people removed their children from the schools, they gave up their right to try to control school policy. They were just in the way, blocking progress.

Vernon felt he made a little bit of progress. By letting it be known that all hiring decisions might be subjected to his very public scrutiny, he was able to raise the proportion of black teachers in the county from less than 40 percent to just about 50 percent. He oversaw preparation of the first formal, written disciplinary code. Most of what he hoped to make happen couldn't possibly happen in a school district that was dirt-poor and growing poorer, but he did intervene a couple of times to see that long-standing maintenance problems in some of the older school facilities, such as contaminated well water, were finally attended to.

In 1982 Vernon Bradley ran for reelection and lost. Turnout in the white precincts was much higher that year than it had been in 1980, and he gathered that white interest seemed to center on the upcoming retirement of East Chestnut High School's white principal. Vernon had made no secret of his interest in hiring a black man or woman as principal, and it appeared that at least in the privacy of the voting booth, the white citizenry left no doubt as to where they stood.

But the same white precincts in which Vernon got clobbered somehow didn't yield so many votes in any of the other races. And Vernon's margin of defeat was just eighteen votes. Furthermore, although all the polling places were equipped with voting machines, the tally in the school board race was delayed and delayed and not publicly released until two o'clock the next morning—more than seven hours after the polls had closed.

Kendrick and his mother Veronica were among the first and most persistent of the many voices crying foul. But Vernon never wavered from his immediate decision to concede and get on with his life. *If they feel so strongly against me that they'll rig an election,* he explained, *there's no telling what they might do if we try to push them to the wall.*

Besides, he had a business to run. He and his wife and sister, joined by Kendrick after he finished high school, had managed to put together a copy shop using rented copy machines set up in a borrowed storefront. Business was steady, but it soon became obvious that to make a go of it they'd have to expand the operation and buy their own equipment. When all the local banks turned down their loan applications, the shop went under.

Two years later they sold their house and used the proceeds to try again, running the shop out of the same trailer they were living in. Business wasn't great, but they began talking to Emily's cousin about franchising the operation so they could expand into nearby counties.

In 1986, after five successful years at the corner of Main and Court Streets in Chowan Springs, Billie's House of Beauty expanded into the former shoe repair shop next door. Billie and Hank knocked out part of the wall separating the new and old buildings, and then between the two front doors they installed a large, modern plate-glass window. The women who were sitting in the chairs at Billie's could look out the new window at the two-hundred-year-old courthouse square, framed by ancient oak trees that shaded the storefronts and offices of all the town's old business establishments. On warm summer days Billie's House of Beauty was a hub of conversation, head-shaking, fundraising, general gossip, and civic activity. It was Chowan Springs's outpost of black social life in the midst of the white town center.

When the remodeling project first got under way, Billie began to make plans for a grand reopening celebration. As the date approached, however, she decided she couldn't handle any big events just then; there was too much going on already at home with her children.

The other night my youngest son went out, and I knew he had a con-

dom. I knew where he kept this one condom, and I looked, and it wasn't there. All I could think was, I should be glad he took it. I better be glad he took it. All I can do is leave him in God's hands and pray for him: "Now, Lord, he's yours, you handle it."

This last boy is such a struggle. He just puts his foot back. But now he says he's going to join the navy, so he'll be seeing some of the things that I have been trying to tell him.

With my niece, too, that's been staying with me, I want her to learn from my own experience. I've done some things that I'm not proud of, and it's not something I really want to talk about either. There's things in my life that I'd much rather they stayed dead forever. But I just decided, it'll all stay dead when I stay dead, and in the meantime, if it'll help this young girl, her heart and spirit, then it's worth opening up the wound.

But she just looks at me and says, "Well, that was you. That was your mistake. I don't have to do the same thing you do." And she says, "Did you really do such and such?" And I say, "Yeah, I did it." And she says, "Well, why is it that you don't want me to do it?" And I say, "If you do it, the Lord will forgive you, but do you think you'll ever be able to forgive yourself?"

And that's exactly where we are right now with my daughter, the one that's married. She didn't do anything wrong, and even so, she still can't forgive herself. She was raped. It'll be six months ago next week. This man who was down from New York, he saw her cutting across the parking lot in back of the feed store, and he pulled her into the weeds and he raped her—right here in Chowan Springs.

He was a complete stranger. That's what my son-in-law can't seem to get through his skull. She knew him—she recognized him, let's put it that way. She knew who he was. But he was a stranger, he wasn't anybody she talked to or associated with or anything like that.

She has just been devastated. She can't even go to work. She goes from *clinic to clinic, pill to pill. She can't live with herself. And she sure can't live with her husband, because I don't think a day goes by that he doesn't bring up how the whole situation has got to be all her own fault. He should be helping her get back on her feet, and instead he's just knocking her down off her feet, over and over again.*

I don't have a whole lot of use for that son-in-law just now. In a lot of ways, he's doing more harm than the man in back of the feed store. I suppose I'll keep praying for the both of them. There's not much else I can think of to do.

Every night during the last week of June, Billie took her daughter and niece to the revival meeting being led by her pastor's son, Reverend W. D. Walker. The young Reverend Walker, it was said, was a rising star. He already had a million-dollar church upstate—or rather, he was fixing to move into a million-dollar church as soon as construction was complete. He was a popular speaker, and the audience grew steadily larger each night. Toward the end of the week politicians showed up to work the crowd, it being June of an election year and only weeks before the primary. In fact, along the pathway between the meeting and the parking lot, Maude Allen and her young people's organization were running a voter registration booth before and after the services. On the Friday night of the revival, Reverend Walker preached on politics and social change; his text for the evening was from the Gospel according to Luke, chapter 9, verse 62: "No man, having put his hand to the plough and looking back, is fit for the kingdom of God."

And today, as a people, are we forging ahead on the path we know will take us into the kingdom? Are we holding our hands to the plough and pur-

suing to the end of the furrow? I suggest to you that we are not—we cannot keep our eyes ahead. We look back over our shoulders at what is being left behind us. Remember: Let the dead bury the dead! We have a crablike mentality, scurrying this way, that way, sideways, backwards. A crablike mentality, with our sights set low to the ground. We must climb out of our shell. We must slough off our crablike mentality. And only then will our people be fit for the kingdom of God.

Do you believe in the word of the Lord? How truly do you believe in the word of the Lord? Recall the story of our poor old sister whose cupboard was bare, who was down to her very last drop of oil, her very last crumb of flour. And she sacrificed her oil, she sacrificed her flour, she put them together and made an offering with them. She made a cake. And she brought that offering, that cake, to her preacher, and she left it in his house, so he would not go hungry.

And the Lord blessed her. The Lord blessed her, because she made the sacrifice when her cupboard was bare. And the Lord will bless you in your congregations, every one of you, if your preachers come home and find oil in their lamps and flour in their cupboards. The Lord will bless a people who see to it that their preachers do not go hungry.

Did you hear that? Shantee Owens was so angry she kept slamming her foot on the accelerator, running the car up to seventy, eighty, ninety miles an hour on dark and winding country roads. *How selfish and manipulative! What good can that kind of blessing bring, in a community that's got no more oil left in their lamps? That's not a blessing, that's a hustle. One thing's for certain. The problems of these people in the twenty-first century are not going to be solved in the church. I felt like a hypocrite being there in the first place.*

In point of fact, Shantee's presence at that particular revival was indeed arguably hypocritical. Aside from whatever spiritual terrain she may have been exploring, she was at the moment venturing into political territory, having filed as a candidate for the Democratic nomination for the office of Chestnut County register of deeds. She worked the crowd at the revival just like so many other candidates—and there was quite a swarm of candidates that summer of 1986. Two of the five seats on the Chestnut County Board of Commissioners were being contested by people Shantee knew: Jerome Harris, her father's nephew from Rosedale, and James Waddell, an old high school classmate of hers who now ran the Texaco station in Chowan Springs. Over in Powell County a young lawyer named Arthur Valentine was running for the state legislature in a district that included six counties and part of a seventh. In both Powell and Chestnut, new candidates were running for so many seats in nonpartisan school board races that both school boards could conceivably become majority-black. Most of the candidates had put in an appearance at the revival.

Did you hear what he said about forefathers? That whole man-woman business—are you a real Christian woman? The woman's place is in the kitchen and in the church, the real Christian woman goes in her pantry and puts everything she's got into a brown paper sack and hands it over to the preacher. Fries him a chicken while she's at it, and then hands over her paycheck and everything else. And meanwhile, the men are supposed to be the leaders, the great wise forefathers, and the women just follow along and do what they say. I've heard that one before!

I know where he got it, because I know that man's father—his mother, too, for that matter. The father is pastor at my church. And one of the things I did when I decided to run for office . . . now, I didn't just come back down here and run over to the courthouse, jump into politics. I waited. I learned my way around. I got myself into the rhythm of this place. And so when I did finally decide to run, I went to see my pastor, Reverend Walker, Senior, and I explained it to him, and I asked for his support.

And you know what he said? First he tried to talk me out of it—you know, asking did my husband really approve, did I realize what I was getting myself into. And then he told me that my big problem was going to be the women in the community—the "other women," I think that's how he put it. They wouldn't want to support a woman leader, there would be jealousy and so on. But then he said something kind of the opposite. He said women weren't political, they wouldn't get involved, wouldn't help me out, they wouldn't even vote, because they were accustomed to the men handling all of that.

I just said thank you, but this is what I have to do. He said he'd help—which he probably won't, but he said he would. Oh, and he said I was my mother's daughter, through and through, an acorn from that tree. I told him I agreed with him on that one, and I said I was sure Miss Orlonia would be in touch with him soon because, of course, she's my number-one campaign manager. It so happens that she's a woman, and she's been the way she's been at least as long as he's been the way he's been. But there was really no point in going into all that with him.

And this is all one of the most frustrating things about being home. That old-timey male country mentality. You have to know your place. You have to smile and hide all your ideas so the men think they're the ones thinking it up. You're not supposed to question authority. It's so stressful really. And especially in politics, the men feel like you shouldn't be there, and if you are there, they just think you don't exist.

And did you ever try to get men to register to vote? The week after next they'll be closing the voter books for the primary, but it's not too late yet. I'd like to take Reverend Walker with me around here when we register people and let him see for himself the difference between the men and the women.

The women will sign up, most of them are glad to do it, but the men—it's like pulling teeth.

> *August 12, 1986.* In Chestnut County, voters selected new-
> comer Shantee Owens, 38, a native of New York, as the
> Democratic nominee for Register of Deeds, over five-term
> incumbent Judith Wiley, 67, registrar at Tri-County Techni-
> cal Community College. Owens, who is married to Anthony
> Owens of Chowan Springs, received 2,788 votes to Wiley's
> 2,637. In November, Owens will face Republican David
> LaBresh, 26, an insurance agent from Rosedale Heights.

The 1986 primary was virtually a clean sweep for the
"newcomers." Shantee, Jerome Harris, and James Waddell all
won their races in Chestnut County and faced Republican
opposition that was not considered a serious threat. In the
school board races, which were conducted like primaries but
involved no party affiliations, one "newcomer" in Chestnut
and another in Powell won clear majorities, meaning that
they were elected with no need for a runoff. Two other black
candidates in each county qualified for the runoffs; they
placed first or second in the voting for their seats but did not
amass an absolute majority. Some had come quite close, however, and their prospects for the runoff looked good. Perhaps
most exciting of all, Arthur Valentine beat three white candidates in the state senate primary, and no Republican had filed
to run against him. All over the region voter turnout was strik-
ingly high for a year with no presidential or statewide races.

James Waddell's race was of special interest to Shantee.
She'd known James since they were kids, and she'd made a

point of looking him up after she heard he sold a fleet of cabs up north to buy the Texaco station in Chowan Springs. From the day he set foot back home he was up-front about his political ambitions, and he talked endlessly about the reforms that were needed, the new programs he wanted to start, the industry he'd bring in, the new services. People started hanging around the station and listening, and after a while the general opinion in town was that James was on a mission. James Waddell had come home to save Chowan Springs from itself. Few people shared his confidence that it could be done, but if the man was willing to throw himself into the lion's jaws, his neighbors were certainly willing to watch and cheer him on.

James campaigned thirty hours a day, ten days a week. He pledged to bring in industry, to transform the industry that was already there by creating employee ownership opportunities, to bust the political process wide open. He'd get roads paved, he'd build schools, he'd even bring a hospital to Chestnut County. James Waddell won his seat on the county commission by the largest margin in any race on the ballot.

Shantee had tried to warn him—but what did she know? Why should he listen to her? She understood that other people tried to warn him, too, but he evidently didn't want to listen to them either.

James meant so well. But he hadn't done his homework, he hadn't learned what it was you can and can't do in political situations. The type of person he is, he just had to find out the hard way. He'd made so many promises, to the point where people expected an overnight turnabout from the bottom to the top, from having nothing to having everything. And he couldn't deliver. You can't do all that much really, especially not overnight.

We're just a little county full of poor folks——we can't pave everybody's road tomorrow. People think it's just because those old white commissioners didn't want to do right, but wanting it isn't enough. We gotta pay for those roads, and where's the money coming from? As a matter of fact, even if we've got the money, it's still got to go through the whole state procedure and get on the highway list. There's more miles of red tape than there are dirt roads, I can tell you that for sure.

People expected so much from James. They thought he had the power and the contacts and the mentality. But when he couldn't deliver, they turned on him just like that. It was all so public——it was embarrassing really. He'd promised everybody about the hospital, and he got this planning committee appointed, and he was the chairman, he had all these hearings around the county. And then the money didn't come through, and everybody just lit on James. They said he was all show, he hadn't accomplished a thing. They didn't see him at all as somebody out there fighting for them. Not anymore. It was like he was on the other side of the fence now.

What I see in all this is that a politician can't do it all alone. It takes a community to change a community, not a politician.

In 1987 Shantee served on the planning committee for a regional conference, cosponsored by MAC, Inc., on economic prospects for rural women. Leaders of public-interest and advocacy groups spent the weekend at the Chowan Springs Holiday Inn to share information on urban development, credit unions, employee ownership, legal services, community colleges, rural health services, and small-business cooperatives.

In 1988 Shantee Owens edged past James Waddell in the Democratic primary race for his seat on the Chestnut County Board of Commissioners. In the general election in November she narrowly defeated a white electrical contractor who had switched to the Republican party two years earlier, after James had trounced him in the Democratic primary.

In Chestnut County the commissioners control a few patronage jobs around the courthouse: several groundskeepers and secretaries, a bailiff, the clerk of the court. When Shantee learned that Vernon Bradley, whose two years on the school board were all but forgotten, wasn't doing so well with the copy shop in his mobile home out on the highway, she arranged to have him named clerk of the court. One day Vernon was sitting at his desk in the courthouse reading through a stack of papers when an old white man he'd never seen before stuck his head in the door of his office and said, *Well, I never.*

Pardon me? said Vernon.

The man shook his head. *Did you ever think to see the day?*

Vernon said, *See what day?*

Well, did you? Did you ever think you would see the day when . . . you know what I mean.

Vernon did know what the man meant, but he said, *I'm sorry, but I don't know what you're talking about.*

The man said, *Well, I'll tell you some time,* and he turned around and walked on down the hall.

Afterword

Elaborating the contrasts between city life and country life—between the Bronx and Burdy's Bend—is a centuries-old American intellectual pastime. The runaway slaves crowded into basement apartments at the Philadelphia end of the Underground Railway must have whiled away many a winter's evening comparing and contrasting. City folk have refined this line of thinking over the years, though the people back home have also indulged in the habit, often framing the dualism biblically: Sodom and Gomorrah out there, God's Own Country around here.

In this old dichotomy, the city is where the money is—and where the strangers are who are liable to cheat you and rob you and lead you astray. Out in the country, they say, people are simple and poor but honest and decent; anyway, they're all your own kin and neighbors, not strangers. For African Americans, the rural South put a cruel spin on this dichotomy: Burdy's Bend was the sort of place where people were robbed and cheated and beaten and shot; New York City was the refuge to which they might flee in times of hunger or peril.

But even this brutal irony couldn't knock the legs out from under the old dualism. The road to the city was still the road to depravity; many a good boy from the backwoods of Chestnut County, we've all been told, was tempted from the path of righteousness when he stepped out onto the streets of Harlem. And many a country girl, in song and story, lost her virtue and everything else in the company of strangers. If only they'd stayed home . . . but they couldn't stay home.

Other American mythologies view the same transformations through different lenses. We are a nation of immigrants, remaking ourselves in the American image, abandoning the ways of the Old Country and taking up baseball. We are a nation of pioneers, restless and rootless, lighting out for frontier after frontier. We never ever stay put, not even after we reach the city; the energetic and ambitious among us become traveling salesmen and corporate transferees, forever young and upwardly mobile and on the road again. We go where the money is, whether we are pushed there by the hard winds of fate or pulled by the glimmer of gold.

The one place we don't go is home again.

At the end of the twentieth century, it is no longer always

easy to tell where the money is—or where home is, for that matter. Where are the jobs? The young people from Burdy's Bend and New Jericho kept on heading north for a decade or more after the jobs disappeared; the migration had acquired a familial momentum that took the better part of a generation to reverse.

But even if those young people had the wrong idea about where to migrate, at least they knew where they came from. Not everyone does in the postmodern world. Many millions of Americans lack a place to go home to. Their families are no longer rooted in a particular piece of American ground, or never did put down such roots. Generations of migration have taken their toll.

Rootlessness is but one of the many costs of migration. Marriages are strained beyond endurance, children are torn repeatedly from their friends and their nest, generations are scattered, never to meet again. The community of trust supporting civil society is undermined; social capital is squandered. Efforts to maintain love and friendship and ordinary neighborliness must be started all over again from scratch. The toll is paid in the old homeplace as well as in the new town up the road, and individuals and families and communities continue to pay the toll for many years—probably even after scores of years.

With the old migration destinations stripped of their promise and the old homeplaces devastated and declining—if indeed home can still be identified at all—is there any difference anymore between one place and another? No one would ever mistake the Bronx for Burdy's Bend, but there is a sense in which the social distance between the two places has been shrunk, much as the geographical distance was reduced to a few hours' drive on interstate highways and eight-lane turn-pikes. Neither place now is clearly the scene of economic opportunity, and both places are sites of danger and insecurity.

What is closing the gap between the poles of city and country? In part, it is migration itself: after a century in which people have moved out and about, the roiling shifts of population have carried ideas and experiences from one American place to another. Most recently the tides have brought millions of northerners and midwesterners, black and white, to the Sunbelt, where they have changed the face of the South. Even sparsely populated places far from the new crowds—even Powell and Chestnut counties—feel the changes, at least indirectly, as state governments reach directly into the global economy. Powell and Chestnut's own people are moving back, bringing home citified ways of thinking about things and doing things, reshaping country life in an urban image.

The old rural-urban dichotomy is based on the nonsensi-cal proposition that rural life—"traditional" society—pro-ceeds outside of history, in a timeless realm of grace. You can't go home again because, like Adam and Eve, you can't get back to the Garden; the real world, the urban, modern world, ensnares you and sullies you.

But people are going home again. And however large the distance between Burdy's Bend and the Bronx, that distance is nothing compared to the gap between Burdy's Bend and Eden. Not a one of the people returning would ever confuse the two. No one is seeking timeless paradise; and no one, however nostalgic, is really seeking to turn back the clock, to return to the Burdy's Bend of segregation and starvation. What people are seeking is not so much the home they left behind as a place that they feel they can change, a place in which their lives and strivings will make a difference—a place in which to *create* a home.

Back home again they will learn right away, if they don't know it already, that they'll need a lot of help to create much of anything out of Burdy's Bend. They'll need one another. In a small country community, people have always turned to one another, but in times past such neighborliness was often hostile to reform. People who have always lived close together, who have never lived among strangers or apart from their friends and family, find it excruciating to spurn that intimacy and maintain the emotional distance required to challenge old ways of doing things. In this regard, the people coming home nowadays are more like strangers than homefolk; another way of putting it is that they are very much like migrants moving someplace new. The city may have been a school of hard knocks, but most people are not retreating from engagement, not running and hiding back home. Like new immigrants everywhere, they seek one another out, form organizations, build coalitions, and eventually start to shake things up.

You can definitely go home again, Eula Grant told me one afternoon on her porch in Burdy's Bend. *You can go back. But you don't start from where you left. To fit in, you have to create another place in that place you left behind.*

Acknowledgments

I hope this book gives back in some small way the generosity of spirit from which I benefited while writing it. Several fellowships made the research possible: a Guggenheim Fellowship; a Rockefeller Humanities Fellowship and a Rockefeller Changing Gender Roles Fellowship; a year at the Center for Advanced Study in the Behavioral Sciences at Stanford; a Research Council Grant from Duke University; and a Faculty Award from the Duke–UNC Women's Studies Research Center.

For more than ten years John Cromartie and I have collaborated on articles on return migration. His perseverance in weaving ethnography and demography together has kept me intrigued. The statistics that appear in this book are a tribute to his fortitude and patience.

Early on in the project several colleagues at Duke University and the University of North Carolina shared my fascination with the changing social character of the rural South; William Chafe, Jacquelyn Hall, Glen Elder, Carol Smith, John McConahay, and Bruce Payne provided advice and dialogue. No researcher could have a more thoughtful colleague than Sidney Nathans. Florence Glasser led me straight to the center of activity in rural communities.

Several colleagues at the University of California, Berkeley, have provided the warmth and intellectual community that we began our academic lives hoping to find. William Rohwer, dean of the Graduate School of Education, gave the kind of support that makes large institutions humane. Jean Lave's creativity is unmatched. Her ways of thinking have changed mine for the better. Nancy Scheper-Hughes's passion for writing inspired me during our fellowship year at the Center for Advanced Study in the Behavioral Sciences; every year is a vintage year for her humor and friendship. Jean Lave, Kristin Luker, Louise Fortmann, and Meg Conkey responded to early versions of the manuscript. Mary Ryan believed in the project, as did my colleagues in Women's Studies at Berkeley. Gillian Hart and I compared notes on land and labor while walking the hills, and David Szanton fortified our spirit and lent his fine editor's eye. Kristin Luker and Jerry Karabel provided a home away from home where food and thought were inseparable. Norma Alarcon and Ole Drier were helpful participants in discussions about writing ethnography. I am thankful for Troy Duster's skill in creating an environment at the Institute for Social Change so suitable for scholarship.

My collaboration with Linda Burton on an article on kin-scripts contributed to my thinking in the early stages of this study. Gunhild Hagestad taught me about family time and historical time, and together we shared a special part of history. Blanca Silvestrini and Carla Peterson influenced the shape of the book. I have also benefited from collaboration with Katherine Newman on another project. Zack Rogow gave editorial assistance at several important moments.

The careful attention of two research assistants has been invaluable. As someone who herself moved south again, Barbara Taylor added a vital dimension to this study. My hope is that she understands why I was soul-searching in someone else's garden. Charlotte O'Sullivan read my field notes and interviews and helped me see the stories in my field notes and the real life in fiction. I owe a special debt to my graduate students. I am particularly grateful to Kamau Birago, Julio Cammarota, Kathleen Coll, Carol Chetkovich, Ann Ferguson, Karen Green, Jayne Ifekwunigwe, Regina Martinez, Christine Palmer, Amy Scharf, Caridad Souza, Pam Stello, Wendell Thomas, and Maria Yen for their contributions to my thinking and for their own superb scholarship.

I feel lucky for the many friends who have seen me through this project. For two months in the spring of 1994 I was given a writer's dream: a retreat in a seventeenth-century post-and-beam house in the woods near Goshen, New Hampshire. The late-night and early-morning debate I enjoyed in Goshen with Deborah Stone and Jim Morone launched the revision of the book. Back in Berkeley, Peter Evans provided on-the-spot feedback, and Louise Lamphere, as always, has tirelessly responded to all I've written. In Point Reyes Station, Patty Glatt's flexibility and hospitality were critical to the book's completion.

Mary Brown's artful sense of documentary informed my understanding of my narrative. For over thirty years Virginia Heuga has offered her good sense and encouragement. Carol Page skillfully managed my life, James Moseley kept track of important matters, Robert Long shared his humor, and Norman Stein provided support and council.

Sandra Morgen hoisted my spirit at every critical moment intellectually and emotionally. Shirley McConahay ensured my safe passage from North Carolina to California. David Nemec stayed by my side when the going got tough, and Ellie O'Sullivan got tough just in time.

From early years in graduate school to the present, John Stack has taught me, by example, how to stick with an intellectual puzzle; our friendship has been a touchstone on life projects. My sister, Barbara Katzman, has provided humor and love over the years, and my mother, Ruth Berman, has been a coworker by my side, in this project and in every other, for as long as I can remember.

As always, I am deeply grateful to the people in rural communities in the Carolinas who shared their lives and offered their participation in this project.

I am appreciative of Roberto de Vicq de Cumptich's cover design and Elliott Beard's book design.

I have been blessed by talented and generous editors. Ellen Stein's determination and creativity transformed the project.

Scholar, poet, counselor, and friend, I thank her and hope she will work with me again.

Steve Fraser believed in the project all along and helped me dodge fate's stumbling blocks and shooting stars. His critical eye never lost sight of my focus, and I tried never to lose sight of his sense of possibility.

No one believed in this book more or prodded me more than my son, Kevin Stack. Kevin listened carefully, read critically, and often reminded me what the book is about: across generations, if we are lucky, we learn from those we have taught.

Suggested Reading

General Interest

"The Black Belt: The Abandoned South." Series in *Atlanta Constitution*, November 16–20, 1986.

Greene, Melissa Fay. *Praying for Sheetrock*. Reading, Mass.: Addison-Wesley, 1991.

Griffin, Farah Jasmine. *"Who Set You Flowin'?" The African-American Migration Narrative*. New York: Oxford University Press, 1995.

Grossman, James R. *Land of Hope: Chicago, Black Southerners, and the Great Migration*. Chicago: University of Chicago Press, 1989.

Lemann, Nicholas. *The Promised Land: The Great Black Migration and How It Changed America*. New York: Alfred A. Knopf, 1991.

Marx, Carol. *Farewell, We're Good and Gone.* Bloomington: Indiana University Press, 1989.

Moody, Ann. *Coming of Age in Mississippi.* New York: Dell, 1992.

Walls, Dwayne E. *The Chickenbone Special.* New York: Harcourt Brace Jovanovich, 1970.

History

Chafe, William. *Civilities and Civil Rights: Greensboro, North Carolina, and the Black Struggle for Freedom.* New York: Oxford University Press, 1981.

Foner, Eric. *Reconstruction: America's Unfinished Revolution, 1863–1877.* New York: Harper and Row, 1988.

Franklin, John Hope. *Reconstruction after the Civil War.* 1961. Reprint, Chicago: University of Chicago Press, 1994.

Giddings, Paula. *When and Where I Enter: The Impact of Black Women on Race and Sex in America.* New York: William Morrow, 1984.

Gutman, Herbert G. *The Black Family in Slavery and Freedom, 1750–1925.* New York: Pantheon, 1976.

Henri, Florette. *Black Migration: Movement North, 1900–1920.* Garden City, N.Y.: Anchor/Doubleday, 1975.

Jones, Jacqueline. *Labor of Love, Labor of Sorrow: Black Women, Work, and the Family from Slavery to the Present.* New York: Basic Books, 1985.

Levine, Lawrence. *Black Culture, Black Consciousness: Afro-American Folk Thought from Slavery to Freedom.* New York: Oxford University Press, 1977.

McDaniel, George. *Hearth & Home: Preserving a People's Culture.* Philadelphia: Temple University Press, 1982.

Sharpe, Bill. *North Carolina: A Description by Counties.* Raleigh, N.C.: Warren Publishing Co., 1948.

Stack, Carol B. "The Kindred of Viola Jackson: Residence and Family Organization of an Urban Black American Family."

In Norman E. Whitten, Jr., and John Szwed, eds., *Afro-American Anthropology: Contemporary Perspectives*, pp. 303–12. New York: Free Press, 1970.

Trotter, Joe William. *The Great Migration in Historical Perspective: New Dimensions of Race, Class, and Gender*. Bloomington: Indiana University Press, 1991.

Demography

Aiken, Charles S. "A New Type of Black Ghetto in the Plantation South." *Annals of the Association of American Geographers* 80, no. 2 (June 1, 1990): 223–46.

Banks, V. J. "Black Farmers and Their Farms." Rural Development Research Report no. 59. Washington, D.C.: Economic Research Service, U.S. Dept. of Agriculture, 1986.

Beale, Calvin L. "The Ethnic Dimension of Persistent Poverty in Rural and Smalltown Areas." In Linda Swanson and Linda Ghelfi, eds., *The Changing Situation of Rural Minorities, 1980–1990*. Washington, D.C.: Economic Research Service, U.S. Dept. of Agriculture, 1995.

———. "Rural and Urban Migration of Blacks: Past and Future." *American Journal of Agricultural Economics* 53, no. 2 (1971): 302–7.

Cromartie, John. "Leaving the Countryside, Young Adults Follow Complex Migration Patterns." *Rural Development Perspectives* 8, no. 2 (February 1, 1993): 22–27.

Cromartie, John, and Calvin L. Beale. "Increasing Residential Separation in the Plantation South, 1970–1990." In Linda Swanson and Linda Ghelfi, eds., *The Changing Situation of Rural Minorities, 1980–1990*. Washington, D.C.: Economic Research Service, U.S. Dept. of Agriculture, 1995.

Cromartie, John, and Carol Stack. "Reinterpretation of Black

Return and Nonreturn Migration to the South, 1975–1980." *Geographic Review* 79, no. 3 (1989): 297–310.

―――. "The Journeys of Black Children: An Intergenerational Perspective." In Patrick C. Jobes and William F. Stinner, eds., *Noneconomic Migration.* Lanham, Md.: University Press of America, 1992.

Dennis, Sam Joseph. "Black Exodus and White Migration, 1950 to 1970: A Comparative Analysis of Population Movements and Their Relations to Labor and Race Relations." Ph.D. diss., American University, 1984.

Fligstein, Neil. *Going North: Migration of Blacks and Whites from the South, 1900–1950.* New York: Academic Press, 1981.

Johnson, Daniel M., and Rex R. Campbell. *Black Migration in America: A Social Demographic History.* Durham, N.C.: Duke University Press, 1981.

Johnson, James H., Jr. "Recent African American Migration Trends in the United States." *Urban League Review* 14, no. 1 (1990): 39–55.

Long, Larry. *Migration and Residential Mobility in the United States.* New York: Russell Sage Foundation, 1988.

McHugh, Kevin E. "The Black Migration Reversal in the United States." *Geographical Review* 77, no. 2 (1987): 171–82.

O'Hare, William P., et al. *Blacks on the Move: A Decade of Demographic Change.* Washington, D.C.: Joint Center for Political Studies, 1982.

Robinson, Isaac. "Blacks Move Back to the South." *American Demographics* 8 (June 1986): 40–43.

Roseman, Curtis C., and James H. Johnson, Jr. "Recent Black Outmigration from Los Angeles: The Role of Household Dynamics and Kinship Systems." *Annals of the Association of American Geographers* 80, no. 2 (June 1, 1990): 205–22.

U.S. Dept. of Agriculture, Economic Research Service. *Rural Conditions and Trends* 4 (Fall 1993).

International Return Migration

Bilsborrow, R. E., T. M. McDevitt, S. Kossoudjii, and R. Fuller. "The Impact of Origin Community Characteristics on Rural-Urban Out-migration in a Developing Country." *Demography* 24 (May 1987): 191–210.

Boyd, M. "Family and Personal Networks in International Migration: Recent Developments and New Agendas." *International Migration Review* 23 (Fall 1989): 638–70.

Gmelch, George. "Return Migration." *Annual Review of Anthropology* 9 (1980): 135–59.

———. *Double Passage: The Lives of Caribbean Migrants Abroad and Back Home.* Ann Arbor: University of Michigan Press, 1992.

Gonzalez, Nancy. *Sojourners of the Caribbean.* Champaign: University of Illinois Press, 1988.

Gould, J. D. "European Inter-Continental Emigration, the Road Home: Return Migration from the U.S.A." *Journal of European Economic History* 9, no. 1 (Spring 1980): 41–111.

Hondagneu-Sotelo, Pierrette. *Gendered Transitions: Mexican Experiences of Immigration.* Berkeley: University of California Press, 1994.

Hugo, G. "Circular Migration in Indonesia." *Population Development Review* 8, no. 1 (March 1982): 59–84.

Kritz, Mary M., Charles B. Keely, and Silvano M. Tomasi, eds. *Global Trends in Migration: Theory and Research on International Population Movements.* New York: Center for Migration, 1981.

Massey, D. S., R. Alarcon, H. Durand, and H. Gonzalez. *Return to Aztlan: The Social Process of International Migration from Western Mexico.* Berkeley: University of California Press, 1987.

Pessar, Patricia R., and Sherri Grasmuck. *Between Two Islands: Dominican International Migration.* Berkeley: University of California Press, 1990.

Piore, Michael. *Birds of Passage: Migrant Labor and Industrial Societies.* New York: Cambridge University Press, 1979.

Thomas, Hope E. "Return Migration and Implications for Caribbean Development." In R. A. Pastor, ed., *Migration and Development in the Caribbean*, pp. 157–77. Boulder, Colo.: Westview Press, 1985.

Women in Migration. Special issue of *International Migration Review* 18, no. 4 (Winter 1984).

Social Theory

Bachelard, Gaston. *The Poetics of Space.* Boston: Beacon Press, 1958.

Berman, Marshall. *All That Is Solid Melts into Air: The Experience of Modernity.* New York: Penguin, 1988.

Bluestone, Barry, and Bennett Harrison. *The Deindustrialization of America.* New York: Basic Books, 1982.

Clark, David. *Post-Industrial America: A Geographical Perspective.* New York: Methuen, 1984.

Coleman, James S. "Social Capital in the Creation of Human Capital." *American Journal of Sociology* [supplement] 94 (1988).

Di Leonardo, Micaela. "The Female World of Cards and Holidays: Women, Families, and the Work of Kinship." *Signs* 12 (Spring 1987): 440–53.

Dill, Bonnie. "The Dialectics of Black Womanhood." In Sandra Harding, ed., *Feminism and Methodology*, pp. 97–108. Bloomington: Indiana University Press, 1987.

Elder, Glen H., Jr. "Families, Kin, and the Life Course: A Sociological Perspective." In Ross D. Parke, ed., *The Family*, pp. 80–136. Chicago: University of Chicago Press, 1984.

Gergen, Kenneth J. *The Saturated Self: Dilemmas of Identity in Contemporary Life.* New York: Basic Books, 1981.

Giddens, Anthony. *Modernity and Self-Identity: Self and Society in the*

Late Modern Age. Stanford, Calif.: Stanford University Press, 1991.

————. *The Consequences of Modernity.* Stanford, Calif.: Stanford University Press, 1990.

Gilkes, Cheryl Townsend. "Building in Many Places: Multiple Commitments and Ideologies in Black Women's Community Work." In Ann Bookman and Sandra Morgen, eds., *Women and the Politics of Empowerment: Perspectives from Communities and Workplaces,* pp. 53–76. Philadelphia: Temple University Press, 1988.

Granoveretter, Mark S. "Economic Action and Social Structure: The Problem of Embeddedness." *American Journal of Sociology* 91 (November 1985): 481–510.

Hagestad, Gunhild O. "Dimensions of Time and the Family." *American Behavioral Scientist* 29 (July–August 1986): 679–94.

Hall, Robert L., and Carol B. Stack, eds. *Holding On to the Land and the Lord: Essays on Kinship, Ritual, Land Tenure, and Social Policy.* Athens: University of Georgia Press, 1982.

Hareven, Tamara K. *Family Time and Industrial Time: The Relationship Between the Family and Work in a New England Industrial Community.* New York: Cambridge University Press, 1982.

Harvey, David. "Class Relations, Social Justice and the Politics of Difference." In Michael Keith and Steve Pile, eds., *Place and the Politics of Identity,* pp. 41–65. New York: Routledge, 1993.

————. *The Condition of Postmodernity: An Enquiry into the Origins of Cultural Change.* London: Blackwell, 1989.

Plath, David. *Long Engagements.* Stanford, Calif.: Stanford University Press, 1980.

Putnam, Robert. "Bowling Alone, Revisited." *The Responsive Community* 5, no. 2 (Spring 1995): 18–33.

————. *Making Democracy Work: Civic Traditions in Modern Italy.* Princeton, N.J.: Princeton University Press, 1992.

Stack, Carol B. *All Our Kin: Strategies for Survival in a Black Community.* New York: Harper and Row, 1974.

Stack, Carol B., and Linda Burton. "Kinscripts." *Journal of Comparative Family Studies* 24, no. 2 (Summer 1993): 157–70.

Literature and Culture

Awkward, Michael. *Negotiating Difference: Race, Gender, and the Politics of Positionality.* Chicago: University of Chicago Press, 1995.

Baker, Houston A., Jr. *Blues, Ideology, and Afro-American Literature: A Vernacular Theory.* Chicago: University of Chicago Press, 1984.

———. *The Journey Back: Issues in Black Literature and Criticism.* Chicago: University of Chicago Press, 1980.

Carby, Hazel. *Reconstructing Womanhood: The Emergence of the Black Woman Novelist.* New York: Oxford University Press, 1987.

Christian, Barbara. *Black Feminist Criticism: Perspectives on Black Women Writers.* New York: Pergamon, 1985.

Gates, Henry Louis, Jr. *Colored People: A Memoir.* New York: Random House, 1994.

hooks, bell. *Yearning: Race, Gender, and Cultural Politics.* Boston: South End Press, 1990.

McDowell, Deborah E. *"The Changing Same": Black Women's Literature, Criticism, and Theory.* Bloomington: Indiana University Press, 1995.

Peterson, Carla L. *"Doers of the Word": African-American Women Speakers and Writers in the North (1830–1880).* New York: Oxford University Press, 1995.

Scruggs, Charles. *Sweet Home: Invisible Cities in the Afro-American Novel.* Baltimore: Johns Hopkins University Press, 1993.

Walker, Alice. *In Search of Our Mother's Gardens.* San Diego: Harcourt Brace Jovanovich, 1983.

Willis, Susan. *Specifying: Black Women Writing the American Experience.* Madison: University of Wisconsin Press, 1987.

Fiction

Angelou, Maya. *I Know Why the Caged Bird Sings*. New York: Bantam Books, 1970.

Bambara, Toni Cade. *The Salt Eaters*. New York: Random House, 1980.

Henderson, George Wylie. *Ollie Miss*. 1935. Reprint, Tuscaloosa: University of Alabama Press, 1988.

———. *Jule*. 1936. Reprint, Tuscaloosa: University of Alabama Press, 1989.

Hurston, Zora Neale. *Their Eyes Were Watching God*. 1937. Reprint, Greenwich, Conn.: Fawcett, 1971.

Lester, Julius. *Do Lord Remember Me*. New York: Washington Square Press, 1984.

Morrison, Toni. *Song of Solomon*. New York: Alfred A. Knopf, 1977.

———. *Beloved*. New York: Alfred A. Knopf, 1987.

———. *Sula*. New York: Alfred A. Knopf, 1973.

Naylor, Gloria. *Mama Day*. New York: Random House, 1983.

Toomer, Jean. *Cane*. 1923. Reprint, New York: Perennial Classic, 1969.

Walker, Alice. *The Third Life of Grange Copeland*. New York: Avon, 1971.

Williams, Samm Art. *Home* [play]. First produced at Yale University, 1985.

Index

agriculture. *See* farming

alcohol, as refuge from despair, 4, 15, 38, 84, 87

Allen, Maude, 145, 148, 156–69, 186

All Our Kin (Stack), xii–xiii

Amway, 132–33, 135

ancestors, importance of ties to, 18

anthropologist: fieldwork techniques, 86–87, 149–50; relationship to subjects, 49–50, 164, 168; voice of, xviii–xix

Autobiography of Malcolm X, The, 54–55

banks, lack of support for black community, 184

Beard, Mrs., 147–48

Beasley, Isabella, 123–24, 126, 132–35, 155

Beasley, Rudy, 126, 133

Beatrice, on caring for elderly, 110

Billie, profile of, 19–29, 184–86

Billie's House of Beauty, 27–29, 184

Bishop, Abraham, 86–87

Bishop, Alice, 80–81

Bishop, Daisy, 93–99

Bishop, Eula (Mrs. Al Grant). *See* Grant, Eula (née Bishop)

Bishop, Jimmy, 92–103
Bishop, Joyce, 86–92, 103
Bishop, Leroy, 37–38, 82
Bishop, Pearl: childbirth, 83–84;
    on child-keeping, 103–4;
    child-rearing, 82–83;
    courtship, 79–80, 82; deter-
    mination to stay, 4; dilemma
    of poverty, 15; on Joyce
    Bishop, 87, 103; land owner-
    ship dilemma, 10, 37–38; as
    matriarch, 2; mother of,
    80–81; on return migration,
    15
Bishop, Samuel: character, 4, 83;
    courtship, 79–80, 82; early
    family responsibilities, 81; ill-
    ness and death, 8–10; land
    ownership philosophy, 37–39;
    migratory life, 82–83
Bishop, Saul, 86–87
Bishop, Shirley, 104
Bishop, Tonesha, 94, 103
Black Power movement, 47–48
Blaydon, Mrs., 28
Board of Commissioners, Chest-
    nut County, 161–62, 188–93
Bradley, Emily, 177–84
Bradley, Vernon, 177–84, 193
Bradley, Veronica, 178–79
Brooklyn Diner, 49–50, 171
businesses. See entrepreneurship
Butler, Slim, 49–52, 171

Carla, on caring for elderly, 117
Carolinas: focus of migration,
    xvii; rural poverty of, 18–19,
    40–41
CATS (Chestnut Action for

Teenage Students), 145,
    162–63
Chestnut Christian Academy,
    180–81
Chestnut County Board of Com-
    missioners, 161–62, 188–93
Chestnut Education Circle, 122
childbirth process, 83–84
child-keeping: benefits of, 104–6;
    burdens of, 119, 185–86;
    intergenerational aspect, 46;
    negative aspects, 88–89; and
    parent-child bond, 103–4;
    Pearl Bishop's role, 2, 4,
    82–83, 85–86; response to
    tragedy, 98; response to urban
    dangers, 46–47, 136, 160
children: chores and, 85, 99; fam-
    ily work of, 81–82; home con-
    nection, 46; isolation in large
    family, 88–89, 92; as leaders
    of migration, xiii–xiv, 2–3; as
    political tool, 148; rural home
    as refuge for, 126
child support payments, kinwork
    as, 105
Christianity. See religion
church: hypocrisy of, 186–87;
    sexism of, 188–89. See also
    religion
city life. See urban life
civil rights movement, as catalyst
    for rural change, 5–6, 49, 171
Clayton, on caring for elderly,
    111–12
Clyde's Dilemma, 107–8
Coleman, Alberta, 59–61
community, rural black: day-care
    center campaign, 139–49;

dearth of young adults in, 46; decline in activism, 155; handling of tragedy, 81–82; lack of development, 40–42; lack of politico-economic power, 174–75; migration as catalyst for change, xvi–xvii; organizing campaign, 153–54, 161–69. *See also* economy, rural; poverty; rural life

community center, renovation of, 71–72, 140–41

consciousness. *See* soul searching

convalescent homes, 112–14, 120

corporate support for rural communities, lack of, 154

country life. *See* rural life

county government: elections for, 188–93; resistance to helping poor blacks, 142–48; and youth group, 161–62

Cromartie, John, 47

Darlene (daughter of Opal), 104

Davenport, Joe, 10–11

day-care services: horrible conditions of, 122–24; rural development of, 134, 139–49

decision-making process for migrants, xv, 19–21, 78, 135–36

demographic profiles: employment, 175–76; migration patterns, 5–8, 45–49

dependency, escaping from, 91–92

domestic abuse, 150–52, 186

Doyle, Vivian, 51

East Chestnut High School, deficiencies of, 179–82

Eastern Carolina Regional Development Council, resistance to new industry, 171–73

economy, rural: changes in, 175–77; decline of, 40; marginal improvements in, 48; stagnation of, xiv–xv, 117; white power over, 6, 174–75. *See also* employment; farming; poverty

economy, urban: northern manufacturing decline, 48; stagnation of, xiv–xv. *See also* employment

education: benefits of, 59, 70, 158, 177–78; importance in recruiting industry, 174; as key to opportunity, 52–55; as leadership developer, 57; pride in, 125–26; of returning migrants, 49; rural schools, 79–80, 179–83; women's advantage, 127, 177; youth group development, 161–63

elderly, caring for, 107–21

elections: black struggles with, 181, 183; county commissioner's board, 188–93

Elsie, on caring for elderly, 114–17

employment: campaign to increase, 172–73; demographic changes, 175–76; lack of security, 196–97; racist politics and, 142–43; as road to dream fulfillment, 24; rural problems with, 3–6, 11–15,

employment (*cont.*)
26–27, 38, 120, 128–29,
135–37, 144; as source of
self-respect, 67, 69; unbearable
working conditions, 72–76;
urban difficulties, 52–55,
158–60; urban rewards, 93,
134
Employment Security Commission, 175–77
entrepreneurial activities: Billie's
House of Beauty, 27–29, 184;
copy center, 178–79, 184
entrepreneurship, 27–29, 70,
132–33, 178–79, 183–84
exploitation, in cities, 130, 132

family networks: Bishops as
model for, 2, 93; caring for
elderly, 107–21; children's
responsibilities, 81–82; geographical separation, 5; Jimmy
and Joyce Bishop, 92–93; land
as focus for, 30–32; maintenance in migration, 7–8;
migration's negative effects, 16,
48, 196–97; migration work
as support for, 104–6,
133–35; parental worries,
184–85; rebuilding in South,
14–15; response to illness,
80–82, 99–103; role in
tragedy, 85–86. *See also* child-
keeping; kinship; kinwork
family values, rural, 99–100
Farmers Home Administration
(FHA), bureaucratic catch 22,
32–37
farming: black participation in,

43–44; bureaucratic frustrations of, 32–37; difficulties of,
5–6, 14, 39; influence of
memories, 20, 28–29; maintaining over generations, 111;
and target migration, 84–85.
See also land ownership
federal aid, need for, 143,
153–54
financial planning in community
organization, 167–68
Fine, Mr., 54
Flats, The, xii–xiii
FmHA. *See* Farmers Home
Administration (FHA)
Fountainhead (Rand), 53
friendship networks: as community service base, 123–24; in
day-care campaign, 145; Eula
Grant and Shantee Owens,
12–13; helping with tragedy,
81–82; Sammy Bishop and Joe
Davenport, 10–11; strength
of, 138–39
fundraising: for CATS, 162; for
day-care center, 146–47; need
for government aid, 153–54

Gabriel, farming frustrations,
32–37
Gamble, Aleisha, 131
Gamble, Collie Mae, 123–24,
127–31, 135–36, 155
gender discrimination: and caring
for elderly, 109–11, 116; religious sexism, 188–89;
women's lack of power, 121.
See also women
generational relations: caring for

elderly, 107–21; migration's effect on, 46. *See also* child-keeping

geography: families stretched over, 7; profile of black migration, 47

government funding, community need for, 143, 146–47, 153–54

grandparents, caring for, 107–21

Grant, Al, 6, 15

Grant, Eula (née Bishop): birth of, 82; character of, 149; child-keeping, 104; and day-care campaign, 145; grief over son's death, 12–15; on Pearl's parenting, 85; return home, 4–5; work and community life, 71–78, 140–41

Grant, Sammy, 10–12

Hampton, Brenda, xiii

Hank and Billie, adjustment to rural life, 19–29

Hardy, Donald, 49–61, 170–75

Harris, Jerome, 162, 196

hatred, destructive nature of, 57–58. *See also* white folks

heirs property, legal problems of, 44

Hines, Tilly, 119

Hines, Wilma, 117–21

Holding Hands, development of, 122–23, 139–40

home: appeal of, 7–8; childhood house, 22–24; complexity of concept, xv; loss of concept, 197–98; meaning of, xiv–xvi, 17–18, 156; as place of

change, 198–99; postmodern interpretation, 196–97; religion as, 21; as source of identity, 78; as spiritual haven, 60–61; statistical profile, 18–19

housing, rural, 23–25, 29–32, 49, 51, 63, 83, 134–35

Hydrick, Clarence, 63

Hydrick, Earl Henry, xvi–xvii, 61–71

Hydrick, George, 66

Hydrick, Marianne, 64–65, 68

Hydrick, Sophia, 64–65

identity, migration journey to, 46, 88–92, 127–28. *See also* soul searching

illness: drain on all resources, 96–97; elderly care burdens, 107–21; family network response, 80–82, 99–103; as focus for caring, 80–82

Industrial Development Council, 173

industry: decline of northern, 48; drawbacks to rural locations, 174; recruiting new, 172–73

Jackson, Viola, xii

James, Mrs., 22

Jewish-black relations, 52–54, 90

jobs, search for. *See* employment

Johnson, Nora, 29–32

Jones, Samantha, 175–77

Kennedy, Robert, xi

kinscripts. *See* kinwork

kinship, ties of, xii–xiii, xv

kinwork: balancing with personal goals, 179; caring for elderly, 107–21; structure of, 105–6. *See also* family networks

labor movement, difficulties in rural South, 75–76

land ownership: appeal of, 42–43, 71; black erosion of, 43–44; as family network focus, 19, 31; as independence, 19–25; perils of, 3, 9–10, 14, 32–39, 113–14, 136; pride in, 132; security of, 98; struggle for, 120, 133–35; symbolism of, 2–3, 29–30, 44

leadership: black community's lack of, 57, 174; conflict in community organization, 165–69

life cycle, and migration patterns, 46–47

Little Red Book (Mao), 56–57

Louis, on caring for elderly, 110–11

MAC (Mothers and Children, Inc.): day-care campaign, 148, 152, 192; formation of, 145; internal political tensions, 148, 152, 165–69

McKinney, Mr., 93

Malcolm X, 54–55

Mao Tse-tung, 56–57

Marlene, on caring for elderly, 112–14

marriage: commitment to, 83–84, 96–97; harassment in, 159; role models for, 100–102;

spouse abuse and, 150–52, 186; strains of migration, 19–29, 135–38

migration: children as leaders of, xiii–xiv, 2–3; costs of, 196–97; effects on kinwork, 105; patterns of, 5–8, 34–35, 41–42, 45–49; religion's role in, 76–78; as source of change at home, 170, 197–99; target, 4–5, 82–85, 93–95. *See also* northward migration; southward migration

military, racism in, 55–56

modernism, migrants as victims of, 156

money, sending home of: benefits for Pearl Bishop, 4–5, 94, 104–6; to build homeplace, 133–35; for child-keeping, 118

moral standards, urban vs. rural, 54. *See also* family values

Morrison, Toni, xvi

mortgages. *See* land ownership

Mothers and Children, Inc. (MAC). *See* MAC (Mothers and Children, Inc.)

Mother's Day Banquet, 164–69

North Carolina, rural poverty of, 40–41

northward migration: demographics of, 81; economic reasons for, 2–3, 52–55, 117, 125–26, 176; escape from poverty, 34–35, 129–30; and soul searching, 88–90; tragedy in, 94–98; trends in, xi–xiii, 176

nursing homes, 112–14, 120

Opal (Pearl Bishop's sister), 80–81, 103–4

Open Door Baptist Church, 65–66

Owens, Anthony, 126

Owens, Shantee: character of, 124–25; on church hypocrisy, 187; day-care job, 152; domestic abuse experience, 149–52; friendship networks, 12–13, 75, 123; political career, 188, 192–93; on rural politics, 191–92

parenting. See child-keeping; family networks

Parent Teachers Association (PTA). See PTA (Parent Teachers Association)

Parks, Halliburton, 124, 150–52

Parks, Orlonia, 12–13, 124–25, 150–52

politicians, hypocrisy of, 156

politics: black community involvement, 170–71, 181–82; black struggles with, 77, 174, 188–93; day-care center conflict, 142–48; Eula's experience with, 8; Hydrick's role, 65–66; rural improvements, 48–49; white power over, 172–75; and youth groups, 162–63

population: effects of migration, 41–42; in rural counties, 123

poultry processing plant, work conditions, 72–76

poverty: dilemma of, 15; family as resource in, 101–2; limitations

on caring for elderly, 107; migration as escape from, 34–35, 129–30; in northern cities, 7; persistence in rural areas, xiv–xv, 18–19, 40–41, 51, 177; rural conditions of, 2–3, 23–25, 129; statistical levels, 123, 143

prisons, rural, 50, 66–67

property, real. See land ownership

PTA (Parent Teachers Association), 180–81

pyramid scheme, 132

race relations: Black Power movement's impact, 47–48; and community organization structure, 166; and education, 80, 181–82; endemic nature in South, 2; hiding from racism, 66–67; Jewish-black, 52–54, 90; land ownership and, 32, 43–44; in military, 55–56; in rural manufacturing, 74–75; in rural South, 2, 57–60; and unemployment, 3; in urban areas, 78; urban North vs. rural South, 70. See also white folks

Ralph, on caring for elderly, 109–10

Rand, Ayn, 53

Reconstruction, second, 171

Redeemers, 171

Redemption, second, 171

regional planning, 50, 59, 171–73

register of deeds, elections for, 188

relationships. *See* family networks; friendship networks

religion: and politics, 186–87; as refuge, 89, 92; in soul searching, 76–78; as symbol of home, 19–21. *See also* church

remittances back home: benefits for Pearl Bishop, 4–5, 94, 104–6; to build homeplace, 133–35; for child-keeping, 118

rest homes, 112–14, 120

risk-taking, in going home, 21–29, 178–79, 184. *See also* politics

rootlessness, of postmodern life, 196–97

Rountree, Menola, 122, 145, 164, 166, 168–69

Roy, farming frustrations, 32–37

rural community. *See* community, rural black

rural life: appeal of, 8, 10–11; daily activities, 77; desire to improve, xvii; moral fabric unraveled, 48. *See also* community, rural black; poverty; southward migration

rural-urban dichotomy: merging through migration, 197–99; transformation of, 195–96

school board: elections for, 190; racial politics within, 182–83

schools. *See* education

segregation, persistence of, 59–60

service organizations, day-care center project, 122–23, 139–49

sharecropping, 20, 28–29, 43

Singer, Mr., 52–53

social capital, effect of migration on, 155–56, 197

social networks, rebuilding in South. *See* community, rural black

social reform, 49, 66, 71–76. *See also* community, rural black; politics

soul searching: Billie's search for home, 19–21; and protection of soul, 59–61; religious element, 76–78; Vietnam War influence, 51, 55–57, 62

South: mythologizing of, 17–18; population gains, xiii–xiv

southward migration: of children, 85–86; costs of, 135–36, 164; demographics of, 5–8; economic reasons for, 48; escape from urban life, 95–97, 131–32, 160–61; gathering of families, 14–16, 111; of northern knowledge, 155–56; psychological reasons for, 61, 91–92, 99; reluctance to return, 133; and soul searching, 68–69; surprising nature of, 19; timing of, 93; trends in, xiii–xiv; variety of reasons for, 6–7, 71; Vietnam veterans and, 58

spirituality, haven for soul, 60–61. *See also* religion

state government, day-care center campaign and, 146–47

state senate elections, black victory, 190

storytelling, and understanding migration, xvi

target migration: Jimmy Bishop, 93–95; Samuel Bishop, 4–5, 82–85
timber interests, desire for land, 37–38
trade, importance of having, 93
tragedy, family network support, 81–82, 85–86, 94–98
transformation of self. *See* soul searching

unemployment. *See* employment
Upward Bound, 157
urbanization, lack of progress in rural counties, 41
urban life: abandonment for rural South, xiii–xv; dangers of, 5, 10–13, 94–98, 126, 131–32, 151, 160, 176; deterioration in 1970s–1980s, 48–49; disadvantages of, 6–7; family networks in, 5, 46–47; job progression in, 52–55; loneliness of, 89–91; as prison, 19–21; racial struggle in, 78
urban-rural dichotomy, transformation of, 195–99

Valentine, Arthur, election victory, 190
values, searching for, 56–57. *See also* family values
veterans, Vietnam War's effect on, 50, 58–59, 68–69
Vietnam War: as catalyst for soul searching, 62; Donald Hardy's experience of, 56–57; impact on northbound migrants, 47–48; influence on soul searching, 68–69
violence: domestic, 150–52; in rural area, 185–86. *See also* urban life
voluntarism, decline in, 155–56
voter registration campaign, 162–63, 189–90
voting, black record in Chestnut County, 163

Waddell, James, 190–92
wage pressure, and white resistance to new industry, 173
white folks: compartmentalizing, 60; debate on seeking votes of, 66; economic power of, 6, 174–75; as exploiters, 72; fear of, 90, 121, 154, 162, 183; greed for land, 37–38; hatred of, 9, 57–58, 77; land as bulwark against, 32; maintaining low profile, 62; majority after northward migration, 41–42; northern attitudes, 52–55; political power of, 5–6, 166–67; resistance to black activism, 142–48, 153–55, 171–73; surprise at black political victory, 193; suspicion of, 2
Williams, Donald, xiii
women: as family foundation, 33; flexibility of, 25–26; wisdom of, 168–69
work, value of, 38, 67

working conditions, rural, 72–76.
   See also employment
Worldly Women, 122

youth: deficiencies in rural education of, 179–82; employment
search difficulties, 176–77;
organizing of, 159–63

Z. Smith Reynolds Foundation,
   142